I'M NOT AFRAID OF YOU

I'M NOT AFRAID OF YOU

ANNETTE MURCOTT

Copyright © Annette Murcott 2020

All rights reserved. This book may not be reproduced in whole or part, stored, posted on the internet or transmitted in any form by any means, electronic, mechanical, photocopying, recording or other, without permission from the author of this book.

Cover image Pixabay

ISBN: 978-0-6488584-0-9 (pbk) 978-0-6488584-1-6 (ebook)

A catalogue record for this book is available from the National Library of Australia

I wrote this book to explain events
because I myself found it hard to understand
how they could have taken place.
If my story helps one person, then it was worth telling.
But mainly this is for my best friend – my son.
And for my family who were also
victims in this injustice.
Some names have been changed to not only
protect the innocent but the guilty too.
This dedication not only goes to my son
and family, whom I love dearly, but also to
the following people for believing in me:
Michael Collins, Sylvie Blair, Aisling Brady and to
all my friends – they all know who they are.
Everyone who supported me through all this.
Thank you so much.

CHAPTER ONE

Journey to Hell

At six in the morning they came for me. The three-day road trip from Port Hedland to Perth was a winner, first class all the way. The cold was extreme. They must think you're like meat, they had the air con cranked right up. This big Ames security truck was like a safe on wheels. The bench seat was too cold to lie on so I lay on the steel floor. There was a lot of anger. I didn't know Bandyup prison existed. I cried at times; I was scared. I was curled up in the foetal position trying to keep warm. It was horrible, no smoking on that flight. Those trucks aren't allowed to stop and let anybody out. The chemical toilet was covered by a camera. I was wearing my standard issue maroon tracksuit pants and top. There were no blankets, no pillow. I couldn't see out; I was enclosed in a box. I couldn't see the drivers, the passing landscape, the sky, nothing. K was up north with his dad and I was heading south. I had never felt so lonely. So alone. I felt sick with loneliness. You think any minute now someone's going to come, at the same time you know no-one is going to come. In Greenough I thought any minute someone's going to come and say this has been a big mistake. But no-one comes. Then you realise that no-one's ever going to come. You feel like you're going crazy, your thoughts spin out of control. I don't know how they can do that to people, and they don't care either. I travelled this way for about sixteen hundred kilometres over those three days. I thought I was going to die. I wanted to die.

It was about nine hours to Carnarvon on the first day, and when we got there, they put me in the lock-up for the night in a disgusting, smelly room on a filthy mattress with a dirty, grey blanket. It was horrific. In the same cell were all the drunks they'd picked up for the night and the smell was sickening. And it was freezing cold. No shower, only a smelly basin with some soap. I couldn't lie on that mattress. I just sat on the concrete floor all night.

The next day I was put back in the truck and we drove to Greenough, the Geraldton prison, almost five hundred kilometres away. I shared a cell with an Aboriginal woman. We didn't speak; I was on the top bunk, she was on the bottom. On the third day we moved on to Perth, four and a half hours away. Before I got on the truck a guard said, 'Hey do you want a book?' It was the Bible and he started laughing. He said, 'Have you read this?' I said, 'Yeah, some poor prick dies at the end of it.' He looked at me and said,

'Whaat?' I don't normally swear but I was pretty much over it all. He just looked at me and then laughed. They thought it was funny. It wasn't at all funny.

The trip was torture. Apart from the cold and discomfort, I wasn't allowed to smoke, so there I was with my bottle of water, my poxy sandwich and an apple or whatever it was in a paper bag. It was total misery.

When we got to Bandyup prison, I wasn't sure where we were. I knew it was in Perth but I couldn't quite place it, I had no idea, I was just in this prison in Perth somewhere.

I got out of the truck and they put handcuffs on me. My hair was everywhere because I had no hairbrush or toothbrush and I'd been in the same clothes for three days. In front of me were two officers, a male and a female. One of them said, 'Well look what we've got here.' I glared at them.

I noticed that the further we got down Australia's west coast, the worse we got treated. The Roebourne officers seemed to be more laid-back, the Greenough ones weren't too bad, but when I got to Perth it was a nightmare. Hell on wheels. They expect you to get off the truck and when they say, 'How're you going, mate, how was the trip,' you're expected to say, 'Yeah, not too bad.' It's insane. It's inhumane. You're supposed to be presumed innocent until you're tried and proven guilty, but on a wilful murder charge you're just a piece of shit to them. Nobody ever gets off that charge so in their eyes you're guilty. They don't have to prove you're guilty – you must prove you're innocent.

They took me into the administration building where they process you and do the paperwork, the same demeaning routine as Roebourne prison. I got to have a shower and they gave me the standard tracksuit, this time blue. I was given a bag of toiletries, a horrible soap, a comb, a toothbrush that looked like it had been stomped on, plus a pair of thongs for my feet.

When you first arrive, they take you to a place called Crisis Care. It's a bit like a hospital. It's quiet and it's clean. They put you in there when you first go to prison; I think it's a precautionary thing in case you want to hurt yourself or commit suicide, and to help ease you into it. You get a better bed and a TV room and a little garden that you can go and sit in and you can also read books. It's just a quiet place. They'd come and watch you, and you had to have a blood test to check for hepatitis, AIDS and so on, you have a medical. I wasn't very impressed; I wasn't in a talkative mood and I wanted to speak to K. I hadn't spoken to him since Roebourne. I was upset, I was crying, I thought I was losing my mind.

The calls to K at Roebourne prison had been hard; it took everything I had not to break down on the phone. It was daunting and it would make me angry. The phone conversations were only allowed to be ten minutes long. They went like this:

'Hello.'
'Hello, Mum, how are you? Where are you?'
'I'm just, you know, I'm just in the jail.'
'Why?'
'Just because of what BJ did.'
'When are you coming home?'
'Soon, mate, soon. How's school?'
'Oh yeah, I did this today,' and he'd start talking about stuff.
'I've gotta go 'cos the phone's starting to cut out.'
'Oh. I love you.'
'I love you too.'
'When are you coming home?'
'Soon.'

I'd get off the phone and I'd start yelling, 'Fuck this! Fuck this!' It was draining. It was gut wrenching.

CHAPTER TWO

Becoming Murcott

My parents split up because dad would leave us for long periods. He'd say he was going to work and then he wouldn't come back for a few months. He'd leave us without money or food. When he died, I found out I had eighteen brothers and sisters, some of them the same age as me. He had women all over the place.

His name was Taylor. He was a fencer and a roo shooter so we lived out in the bush when I was tiny, we didn't even have a house. Mum met him when she was sixteen and had her first baby, Dianne, when she was seventeen. By the time I was born, Mum was twenty-five and my father was forty-four. There was a huge age gap between them. My mum's parents owned a big property and her dad died when she was twelve so my grandma was left with a big property and seven kids. My dad came and worked on that property and then took my mum away, and the family didn't see her for a long, long time, even though she had four kids. We lived in a camp situation in tents out in the bush. It wasn't unusual for families in those days to live in the bush and follow the work around but Mum doesn't say too much about it, just that she never had a house with him and he was always off with other women. Mum and he weren't even married. She doesn't remember whether she left him or he left her. She wrote a letter to him and gave it to his brother but he never contacted her.

After Mum and Dad broke up, we went to live with Mum's brother who was a prison officer. He quit after a nervous breakdown from working in Fremantle jail, but had a mate, Mr Murcott, who met Mum through him. When Mum and Mr Murcott married, he adopted my two older sisters, Dianne and Helen, and my brother Ross and me, and so we became Murcotts. We lived in a big house in Mount Claremont. It was owned by Mr Murcott who also had custody of his kids. I was two when they married, Ross was five, my sister Helen was six, my stepbrother Ray was seven, Dianne, my eldest sister, was ten, and there were two older stepsisters, seven children in all, quite a full house. I used to get on quite well with Ray, and Ross and I were close. I was a bit of a tomboy and I'd sit out the front in my board shorts waiting for him to come home.

Ted Murcott was a big man who had no time for us at all. I feared him. He seemed huge when I was so little, and he was a big bloke anyway. He'd been in the SAS (Special Air Service) before becoming a prison officer. We lived in fear of making any noise, or going to the toilet, or sitting at the table, anything really. If Ross or I upset him, we just got a belting, we'd get the thong or a backhander. He never physically hurt my mum or my sisters, and he never laid a hand on his own children, just me and Ross.

Murcott was a bully. Mum wasn't allowed to have much and he'd give her fifty dollars a week to buy food for a household of nine, which didn't go far. He was the money earner. He wasn't very nice to Mum or us, which I was aware of from a very early age. At Christmas time his kids would get lots of presents and we'd get one each. He was nice to his own kids. They were aware of it too. Because Mr Murcott used to belt Ross and me around quite a bit, I never liked to be with him on my own, I never felt comfortable or safe.

Ross remembers when I was about two or three and I wouldn't eat my dinner. Murcott kicked the highchair out from under me and I slammed onto the ground, and then he force-fed me. I was crying and gagging. It was distressing for Ross to watch.

Murcott would also pick me up in my highchair, put me out in the laundry and turn the lights out. He'd smack the shit out of me with a thong, trying to force-feed me. He continued doing it as we got older, and when we were little tots he'd make the two of us go out in the laundry with the dog and would make us eat our dinner out there.

It brings back bad memories when we talk about it and Ross gets angry. I've been a bit angry too lately. It's hard, I've spent many years trying to forget it and push it away, but it's always there. He used to bash me when I was so little. I was a vent for his rage.

Ross used to wet the bed a lot and my stepdad would pull him out of bed and beat the crap out of him, then make him stand in the toilet until he went again, which he couldn't do because he'd already done it. He used to frequently hit Ross. He would hit us with a belt on our backs, or the back of our legs. One of his favourite things when we were little was to grab us and hold us up off the ground and smack the crap out of us. He'd say, 'I'll give you something to cry about.' Now when I think about it, I think: settle down. I could almost laugh, although it's not at all funny. I suspect that now you could go to jail for something like that. For some reason, most of the doors in that house had locks on the outside so he could lock you inside your bedroom or other rooms.

His mother lived there too. They both used to drink all night and she'd piss herself at the dining room table. They'd sit there and drink king browns[1] and when they got drunk they'd get into punch-ups. If you made a noise, he'd get up and give you a flogging. Having said that, he could be nice at times, but only if he'd been drinking. More often

---

[1] King browns – West Australian name for 750 ml long-necked beer bottles, named after the large, venomous snake.

he was nasty and cruel. The best rule was always to stay out of his way. I was always frightened of him. He's on his death bed now and wants to see us to say sorry, but there's no way. We were in fear of him, and being kids, we had nowhere to hide, nowhere to go.

We were sent outside most of the time, which suited us. I was always an outdoor kid. I played with my brother, playing with train sets, making cars, climbing on the roof, just boy stuff. We used to make flying foxes, and go down to the local lake and look for golf balls, or go to the beach and play on skateboards, or build pushbikes and just hang out with mates. We played with the neighbour's kids and we got up to a bit of mischief, like making chlorine water bombs, just stuff that would annoy the neighbours, but we had no trouble with the police or anything. We were too scared of what Mr Murcott might do if he found out, and all the neighbours knew us, the kids from Rochdale Road. There was always something going on, which made those parts of life enjoyable. We had a lot of friends around that neighbourhood, and there were always lots of people at the house. Remember, there were seven kids, so if we all had a friend over that was fourteen kids! It was flat out. I have to laugh, when I think about it I feel sorry for my mum.

Five o'clock was dinnertime and if you were late you knew you'd get a smack, and if you did anything wrong you'd get clouted by Murcott. If Ross or I didn't eat our dinner, he'd make us sit there at the kitchen table until ten thirty at night. We couldn't move until we ate it. So, five hours later we'd be sitting eating cold potato or whatever it was that we didn't like. Or sometimes I'd get up to get a drink of water after I'd stuffed the food into my cup and then I'd get rid of it down the sink.

There were lots of things we couldn't do. If you farted in the lounge room you didn't dare look at your brother – this is a funny thing when you're little, but if you sniggered at it you'd be banned from the lounge room and from watching TV for a week. Stupid stuff, but I can laugh at it now, it was just so ridiculous. The fact that I can laugh is a bit sad, I think. If it was pouring with rain he might, when I was older, offer me a lift to the shops or my friend's place, but I always refused; I didn't like being alone with him.

Mr Murcott was a hard, cruel man, and my mum never did anything about it. When I talk to Mum about it, she says at least he put a roof over our heads, and there was no welfare money in those days. She just thought she was doing the right thing and so she put up with it. I could never imagine doing that. Me, I'd rather take K and live in a cardboard box than watch someone abuse him. Dianne, Ross and I talk about it now and we still don't understand what our mum was thinking. My brother was so protective towards me and gets upset talking about it, saying, 'I couldn't do anything about it because I was only a couple of years older than you.' He feels guilty, but there was nothing he could do.

I don't remember any arguments between Mum and Mr Murcott. I also don't remember ever being cuddled or played with or read to by Mum. Dianne tells me that in the mornings I never went and jumped into bed with Mum, I always jumped into my sister's bed and she'd read me stories. Maybe we weren't allowed to, I don't know. Because the abuse started when I was so little, I suppose I just thought that this was the way things were. I never discussed it with friends, although I never wanted to go home after school.

Mum finally left Murcott for good when I was eleven, so this abusive life went on for nine years.

My sister got married about six years ago. My stepbrother was there and I hadn't seen him for a long time, but we were happy to see each other. He asked me when I was going to visit Dad. I said, 'What are you talking about? He's not my dad.' He said, 'I know he was a bit cruel but you should forgive him, he wants to see you.' I said, 'Forgive him? You have no idea. He was your father, he never hit you, you were spoiled.' Now he wants me to go and visit him and to give me some old photos. Does he want to say sorry because he's sick or dying? I'm not interested.

CHAPTER THREE

Escape and Electrocution

I came home from school one day when I was about nine or ten and all our stuff was packed up. I don't remember there being any arguments, but his heavy drinking was a bit of a problem. My mother never drank, smoked or even swore. Mum had met him through her brother who was a prison officer.

Knowing we were leaving left me feeling somewhat confused, but also happy. I remember moving to another house, but I had no feelings of sadness. Maybe because I felt I had Mum to myself now. Mum had been at home with us kids until we got older and then she became a marriage counsellor. Before they broke up, Mum had been going out quite a lot with her work. Mr Murcott had always controlled the money and he didn't want her to work outside the house. I'd see her crying sometimes, but if she was unhappy, she hid it well. I don't remember there being lots of arguing, I just remember that we left. He didn't want her to go.

There was another man living with us in the house we moved into but I can't recall whether that was six months later or twelve months later or whether he'd been on the scene all the time.

My main memory of that period was sometime later, the day I got electrocuted. The house we'd moved into was an old high-set house, a bit like a Queenslander. We used to get up on the roof to watch the Royal Show as we were right by the showgrounds. There was only room for one on the roof; the other would have to climb the tree. So, we'd get up there maybe a week before it opened and watch them training. One day I came home from school and everything was live – even the tap would give you a zap. It was my turn to sit on the roof and my brother's turn for the tree, so I stood on the back steps and jumped up to grab the guttering. It was full of electricity and all the voltage that was going through the house went through the bottom of my foot and kicked me backwards where I smashed my head on the backyard bricks.

Mum had just pulled into the driveway from work and she raced over to find me without a heartbeat. She gave me CPR while my sister ran next door to get them to phone an ambulance as we didn't have a phone. Mum managed to revive me before the ambulance arrived. The knock to my head left me with a concussion. They said I'd rattled my brain. Mum tells me that in the hospital on my way to X-ray I said to her, 'I'm never going to be the same again, am I, Mum?' and she said, 'You never were!' I was raced to the Princess Margaret Hospital and when I woke up Mr Murcott was there. Maybe Mum needed a shoulder, but there he was and we moved back into his house. I never can remember those years in between leaving and then moving back into that house – that's all gone except for the electrocution.

A couple of days before, the power line had come away from the house and was hanging from the power lines onto the roof. My mum had rung the power company and they sent an apprentice who had fixed it, but he'd mixed up the wiring and crossed them over on the meter box, from memory. Anyway, he hadn't fixed it properly so the house was live. You couldn't touch anything metal like the washing machine or the kitchen taps. When I grabbed the guttering, I couldn't let go of it. It was direct current. The only way I can describe the feeling was like the vibration you'd get hanging onto a jackhammer. The current came through my hand and out my foot which jolted me off the roof and onto the concrete.

I was in hospital for a week, and every time I woke up, I'd vomit. When I got out, I just went back to my tomboy activities. And of course, we were back at Mr Murcott's place, I don't know how long for. I don't remember being there at all, it's all gone. I don't remember anything at all until we moved out of Mr Murcott's again and into another house in Swanbourne, a suburb in Perth.

I was about eleven when we left Mr Murcott again. My mother was now with a new man. In between him and the previous one she was lonely and I spent a lot of time with her. She cried a lot. She didn't have much money and she had all of us kids with her. She was still working part time as a marriage counsellor and she also had a cleaning job for a big day-care centre in Nedlands, a wealthy suburb in Perth. But loneliness was her biggest problem.

I was one of those kids who got on well with people and at school I hung around with lots of different groups, even when some of these groups didn't get on with each other. Even now I have a lot of different types of friends who don't necessarily like each other.

Maybe this is because I was brought up in a large family, but I've always had the ability to know what's going to happen. It's a strange thing and difficult to explain, but it annoyed a previous partner when I'd tell him what was going to happen to him during his day. Watching the rugby with my brother one day, I said to him, 'I bet that ball's going to hit me in the face,' and a few minutes later it did. I knew I was going to get cancer too and I also knew that I wasn't going to die from it. Maybe it's some sort of insight.

I've been like this as long as I can remember and my sister's the same, although she doesn't have it as much now. It seems to be handed down as my son K is the same.

We'll be driving down the road and he or I might say, 'Oh, there's going to be a police car coming after this truck,' and there it will be. When K got a new Commodore a while back, he said to me, 'I had a dream that when I went down to Perth I got a yellow sticker put on my car,' and he rings me up two hours later and says, 'Mum, I got a yellow sticker put on my car.'

Sometimes this knowing comes to me in dreams, like the death of my ex-partner's aunt, which happened four days after I dreamed someone in his family was going to die. But usually it's just a feeling, a knowing. It's good in that it protects you from people who wouldn't be good to have in your life. I get a strong sense about people when I meet them.

CHAPTER FOUR

Swanbourne

When we moved to Swanbourne, I was just about to start high school. I wasn't too excited about the idea; it was a big high school and Ross warned me not to come near him and his mates there. I'd respond by telling him I was going to come and hold his hand and he'd tell me if I did that, I'd be dead. I had a few primary school friends moving on to Swanbourne High with me.

On my first day, I put on the white blouse, the long pleated skirt and the sandals that made up the girls' uniform. I wasn't too happy about it as I wasn't a girly-girl and wasn't used to wearing skirts. I walked down the hill to the school on my own feeling quite nervous. Overwhelmed by the number of people when I got there, I spotted some friends and we all ended up in the enrolment room, about thirty of us. It was Mr Mast, the art teacher, who was doing the enrolment, and when he called out 'Murcott!' I replied. He looked up at me and said, 'You're not related to Ross, Helen, Dianne, Ray, Ruth and Ruby, are you?' I said, 'Yeah,' and he said, 'God, how many more of these are there?' I told him, 'I'm the last one, I'm the seventh.'

I was happy that Ross was there, even though he'd told me to stay away from him. He and his mates looked out for me, so I felt protected and I soon made new friends and fitted in quite well. There were a lot of rich kids who lived in big houses with nice stuff in good suburbs like Cottesloe, and as we didn't have much and Mum was working and struggling to pay the rent and buy food, I didn't want them to come to my place, so I'd go to theirs. We didn't have a horrible house but it was nicer at their homes. They didn't treat me any differently.

My best friend was a girl from Kenya called Bella. I'd been friends with her in primary school where none of the kids would talk to her because they had never seen anyone who looked like her: dark skin, frizzy hair, long skinny body. She lived with her father who was white, while her African mother lived back in Kenya. I started to get to know her and went to her house one day where her farther told me she used to come home crying every day, so he told her to go to school and be something they'd never seen before. So she would hold her bottom lip out and do this high-pitched whistle. We carried on being good friends through high school. School was good – it was a bit like a big happy family.

I was good at school in the beginning, especially in maths and science, but I didn't apply myself, maybe because I hung out with kids who weren't interested in being there. I found things like social studies and history boring, some teacher just rambling on about things I wasn't interested in. My mind was on other things. I started out getting good grades but then I stopped handing things in and was sent out of the class a fair bit. My mum said I was arrogant. I didn't do anything bad but I did spend a lot of time out of the class, usually for laughing a lot and making the other kids laugh – I guess I was disruptive. I didn't take it seriously; I didn't think it was important but, apparently, it was.

I was into sport and was very good at it. I took part in all the sporting events and swimming events and was sports captain. I did little athletics after school. I wasn't into team sports; swimming and running was my thing. I liked beating the boys too. I wasn't a bad loser but I loved winning.

At thirteen I went to school camp for a week and there was Tim, my first boyfriend. He was a scrawny little kid. He liked me and I liked him, but when we got back to school he was grinning at me one day when I was up on the balcony and he was down below. I chucked choc milk on him because I didn't want him to like me or for anyone to know I liked him. I had lots of boys who liked me but I wasn't too keen on the idea. I couldn't work out why they liked me. Maybe I developed quite early. Anyway, Tim and I were like childhood sweethearts for a couple of months through high school and he used to ride his bike two miles to come and see me and Mum got to know him. I don't think I was very nice to him. I was too busy doing my own thing and preferred hanging out with my brother and my mates, and I suppose I was just too young and didn't care.

When I was in high school, I always thought I'd like to work with animals. I dreamed of working as a park ranger or a vet or something along those lines. I always knew I wanted to do that, but then I moved up to Newman which was a mining town and there's nothing there – it's a closed town meaning you cannot live there unless you work for that mining company. There's no accommodation, nothing, it's for BHP workers only. I never really wanted to get into mining.

When we were young and lived at Murcott's place, we had lots of birds and cats and dogs. I always wanted a dog of my own but was never allowed one, and when I was with K's father, I got a blue heeler. I had him for twelve years and even when K was born he was my best mate. He was something I had always wanted and he was very protective of K. You couldn't have him around other children. His name was Thai, and there was K, his father and me, and he was our dog. He was this rough, rugged dog. He used to jump on the back of the ute, he'd go roo shooting, he was like Red Dog, that dog from Dampier, a hard, strong blue heeler.

Later, when I was with K's father in Pannawonica, there were only about twenty streets in the town. It's also a closed town of Rio Tinto. K was a little baby and I'd held on to my dream and started studying to be a park ranger.

Even now, I'd give up my high paying job for something more to my liking. I don't have much heart for what I do; I do it for the money but it's not fulfilling. I still want to do the park ranger course, but with the interruptions in my life, I suppose doing what I do is the easy way out. Trouble is, the money's there but you're a visitor in your own life. Right now I'm thinking, well, this is good, I've gone back to mining, K and I are on opposite shifts, I'll see him once every six weeks. The thing is, once you start doing two weeks on, one week off, you're so tired and have so little time. You finish night shift, you fly out at seven forty-five in the morning and get into Perth at nine thirty, so your whole day is like a blur, like somebody's drugged you, but you want to spend that day awake so you don't waste it. The second day you're still tired, you start getting yourself together, you might start seeing a couple of people, you see your family, and it's so hard to crowd all that in, just trying to do those few things, and then you go back to work again. It's so hard. It is being a visitor in your own life.

Going back to the story, around that time Mum had a new boyfriend who was a big boss in the Fremantle fuel depot and she wanted me to move to Newman with her to live with him. This was the end of my first year at high school. I asked her where that was and she pointed it out on the map and I laughed. 'No no no, I'm not going there,' I said. I had my school and mates and sport, I wasn't going to have that. I also knew that he was seeing another woman. It was the same with an earlier boyfriend of hers who used to say he'd been in the army and had a farm and was going to give Ross and me all this stuff like motorbikes and I'd say to Mum, 'Nuh, he's lying.' She'd get upset and say, 'You never want to see me happy,' and blah blah blah. I always knew they were telling lies to Mum but she never used to listen.

She knew Dianne and I had this ability to know what was going to happen but she didn't understand it and didn't want to know anything about my experience with it. She may have been frightened of it and she'd say, 'Well if you can read the future, then why don't you know the winning lotto numbers,' and I'd explain that I can't see the future, I just know what's going to happen, I can't see exact times and numbers.

She said that we were moving and that was that. Ross didn't have to go as he was fifteen and had just got an apprenticeship, so that just left me. But first Mum went up there for a holiday and left some sort of carer woman to look after us. I packed my bag for school the next morning and told my brother I was leaving. I must have been fourteen, and so I left, I didn't go home. I stayed with some friends for a couple of weeks. I didn't know Newman and I didn't like her boyfriend and I wouldn't even have Ross up there, and we were close. Also, this man had a son and we didn't get on at all. He didn't want to share his dad and his dad spoiled him.

After a couple of weeks, I decided I should go home and I caught the bus to the local shopping centre where my cousin used to work. When I walked in she said, 'My God, where've you been?' She growled at me and said everyone had been looking for me and the police had been searching for me and that Mum had had to come back from Newman twelve hundred kilometres away when she'd heard I'd gone missing.

CHAPTER FIVE

NEWMAN

So, I moved up to Newman and went to school there until I was sixteen. First, I went up there for a holiday. I'll never forget it. I was there for a couple of weeks and didn't know anyone, so Mum and I just went around doing the tourist thing and it was unbelievably stinking hot. All that red dirt and heat and I knew I wasn't staying there!

Back down to Perth on the bus I went. Later, Mum asked me to come back up for a holiday, which I did, and then I couldn't leave. It was a trick. His son was there and we ended up being friends because we were the same age, in the same class and we lived together. It was where I had to live. But when I first went up there, they may as well have chucked me off the face of the earth; I knew no-one and there was nothing there. I just had to suck it up. For a start, I didn't know where we were, I was just out in the middle of the desert. It's only four hundred kilometres away from Marble Bar, the hottest part of Australia.

Imagine – desert, spinifex, stinking hot, flies, nothing to do, and that's Newman.

It was a closed town and owned by BHP mining. There wasn't normal TV because the shifts used to be something like 6 am 'til 2 pm, then 2 pm 'til 11 pm, then 11 pm 'til 6 am, and the TV was like a BHP network and just played the same shows over and over. The same shows were on from 6 'til 2, then they were repeated from 2 'til 11, then another repeat from 11 'til 6 am. There wasn't even a video shop.

There were maybe forty kids at the school. It was small and hot. I did eventually settle in and made quite a few friends. A lot of the kids up there were like me, very similar in personality, their parents all worked for the mine, we all lived in similar mining houses. After some time, I started losing touch with all my Perth friends – the letters became fewer as I started getting on with my life and they carried on with theirs.

Now I look back on my time there and think it was probably the best time of my life. Even though there was nothing to do, we used to hang out and there was speedway and motocross. I now think that growing up in small towns is the best thing for kids. My own son was brought up in a small town and I can see the difference between small town kids and those brought up in Perth. There's a completely different attitude. In a small town, everybody knows who you are and everybody knows who you belong to, so if you stuff up, you're going to get in trouble anyway. The kids I know who've been brought up in Perth don't seem to have much respect for their elders, grandparents, aunts and uncles, whereas small town kids seem to be well mannered, easygoing and honest. I guess because there's not so much to do, they get more involved with life and must deal more with people. They can't get on a train and go into the middle of the city and run amok and graffiti, or go out until three in the morning and get up to no good, because there is just nothing to do at three o'clock in a small town. I find many Perth kids are quite rude. They weren't raised in a mining town where most people did shift work and you had to be considerate of noise when people were sleeping, for example. In a small community people get on better because you just have to. And you can't just wander out of town, because there's nothing out there.

In Newman, I still only went to school because I had to, nothing changed there. But Mum and her boyfriend broke up; he'd been sleeping with another woman. In Newman, you had to work for the company, and you couldn't rent a house if you weren't employed by BHP. So, we moved in with another bloke who was looking for a housekeeper and Mum cooked and cleaned for him and started studying to become a dental nurse. She'd applied for a job as a dental assistant with a local dentist, never expecting to get the job as she'd never done anything like that before. But the bloke hired her and she wanted to become a dental nurse, so he sent her down to Perth to study. I remember her at exam times stressing and saying she couldn't remember things and she couldn't do it, and I'd tell her she could do it and ask, 'Why do you need a bloke all the time? None of it works out anyway. Why don't you get a job and not have to rely on anybody?' because she used to get hurt all the time.

So she studied and graduated and I was really proud of her. She became a completely different person. She was very pretty and such a nice person, everyone loves her, including all my friends. She's just a nice, decent, caring person, but she just kept on getting shat on all the time. She believed all the lies her boyfriends told her, and when I'd tell her they were telling her shit, she'd say, 'How do you know?' I'd say, 'How do you not know?' I suppose she just didn't want to believe it.

People would tell me they'd seen him with other women in places where he didn't think he'd be seen. After she became a dental nurse, we ended up moving back in with the boyfriend she'd left because he said it was all lies, but then he turned around and did it all over again. And so we moved back out to the other house again. She loved him and even now, although she's now married to another bloke, I think she still loves him. I think maybe if I hadn't been around and maybe if he didn't have a son and if he and Mum had had children together, they might still have been together living happily ever after, I don't know.

I met my son's father in Newman when I was seventeen. I'd left school when I was sixteen – lots of my friends left and I'd lost interest in school and was getting into trouble. All the moving around houses got to me and I didn't like my mum at one stage. I was unhappy, especially when she went back to that bloke I didn't like, so that caused problems. He wasn't a nice bloke and he'd make awful comments. I didn't like being there when he was there, so I spent a lot of time going out. My brother Ross had moved up and was living with us at that stage so that was one good thing. But everything was pretty pear-shaped. Mum knew I was unhappy but she didn't seem to care because she was happy. I felt that I was in the way, really. It wasn't something I could talk to her about because she's one of those people who doesn't like to talk about difficult things; if you try to, she'll just change the subject.

I went to work in a bakery as there weren't any other jobs around, just Coles or IGA. Everybody went to the mine but you had to be eighteen. In the bakery, we just made bread, pizzas, take-aways, things like that. I just packaged the products and served people but I didn't enjoy it. I'm just one of those people who don't like serving people. All the drunk people from the pub would come in at night to get food and would give you a hard time and I just thought, nah, I don't want to be here. But I had to do something because Mum said if I was going to leave school then I had to have a job. And she was single at the time.

And then she met Dave at a party one night. I was friendly with some people who were quite a bit older than me. Jane was twenty-two and was married to a project manager at a mining company called Macmahon's. They invited me to a Christmas party and I took Mum with me and the big boss of Macmahon's was there, Dave, who's her husband now. That was twenty-four years ago.

I didn't like him to begin with either. I just didn't want anyone to be with Mum. I finally had Mum to myself and got to spend some time with her without some arsehole hanging around. I'd say Mum had spent half her life crying. Half her life heartbroken and half her life crying. I didn't like the way other men had treated her, but Dave was completely different to the other partners she'd had. He always used to talk about things I had no idea about, a lot of mining and technical stuff. He and I always remember one conversation we had once when Mum was going down to meet him for lunch. She didn't know him very well and I was walking past and saw them sitting together. Mum called me over and asked me to join them, which I reluctantly did, and while Mum was up getting a coffee, Dave asked me how I was and I said, 'Stay away from my mum. I don't like you, just stay away from her.' He still recalls that conversation. Mum came back with the coffee and asked what was happening and we sat there pretending nothing had happened.

But he didn't stay away from Mum, he just kept on coming back. And it's funny that, because he's the one person in my life that I never wanted to disappoint. I never wanted him to think badly of me. Just thinking about it makes me start to cry. A couple of years later they got married. By that time my attitude towards him had changed. He'd been in the army and mining in Jakarta and been all over the world. He had kids with his ex-wife who he'd broken up with quite a long time ago. He was firm and didn't put up with much. At that stage I'd be having friends over for drinks and he didn't like it. He was a nice bloke but he'd say, 'Look, I'm not putting up with any of your shenanigans,' and he meant it. He wasn't horrible but you'd know not to push the limits with Dave. I had a great deal of respect for him. If I needed to talk to someone it would always be Dave. He was the first man I respected, because he treated Mum really well. He treated us kids well too but that didn't matter so much to me, what mattered was that he was good to Mum.

He could also be funny but it took him a while to warm to us. We'd swear and fart and he didn't like that as he was quite the gentleman, he didn't see the funny side of that. When Ross would come home drunk late at night, and we'd be trying to grill toasted cheese on the toaster outside instead of in the inside griller, we'd wake him up with our noise and he'd come out and blast us, get angry that Ross was drunk again and tell us to shut up and send us to bed. And then you wouldn't get spoken to for days, so you knew not to upset him in that way.

He's completely different now. He's sort of become one of us instead of us becoming like him. Thank God. He's brilliant. And he gave Ross his first job on the mine site and later he did the same for me. But he's also sacked my brother and me. He was the father I never wanted to have, but I'm so glad that Mum stayed with him, he's a brilliant, interesting man. He has a photographic memory so if you ask him something, he'll say, 'It's in that book over there, chapter forty-one, page ten.'

He had always been successful and had high expectations for us. He's now got dementia and Parkinson's at seventy-two. I get quite upset every time I see him. Mum reckons we've got some special connection. Dave and I have always had a lot of time for each other and he's like that with my young son K. I'd always ask his opinion and advice on any decisions I had to make, even if I didn't like what he had to say. He's a good guy.

Sometimes he'd get sent into mining companies to fix them up if they were losing lots of money. He'd say, 'I'm not here to make friends, you don't make a lot of friends when you're the boss.' He said, 'I've sacked family, I've sacked friends, it's hard, but someone has to do it.' I've worked for Dave twice now and you're not treated with any favouritism because you're family. In fact, he's harder on family. He used to tell me that I could do things and go places in my life and that he could get me in the office, and I'd say, 'Your shoes are too big for me to fill,' and he'd say to me, 'You're so much smarter than you make out, but you don't want to go higher up in the workplace, do you? You just want to hang out with your dump truck mates, you just want to be average Joe Blow,' and I'd just say, 'Yeah,' but I think about it now and I didn't really want to, I wanted to be where Dave was at.

CHAPTER SIX

Mining and Marriage

The day Dave sacked me I wasn't at all happy. It was very hard on me. He said, 'Where can we go from this, because I have to do this,' and I said, 'You don't have to do this, I've just done exactly what so many other people have done but you haven't sacked them.' He told me, 'If I don't sack you, they're going to think that I'm favouring you.'

I was shocked. I remember saying, 'Favouring me! You shit on me all the time!' He said, 'I'm going to have to let you go,' and he stood up to shake my hand! I was stunned, and he had tears in his eyes. And I just said, 'Go fuck yourself then, you don't sack me!'

I went back to my room – I was living in the mining camp – and I started packing up all my things. Mum rang and asked me what I was doing. I told her and when she asked why, I explained that I'd blown over the limit. Every morning at work we were breathalysed and that morning

I'd failed it. So had four others as it was just after the Christmas party. I know that there was no excuse for it, but normally they'd just send you home and the next day you'd come back to work.

The next thing, Dave called me and asked me to come back to the office. I reluctantly drove back and he offered me my job back. I told him he'd just sacked me and asked why he'd changed his mind. He told me he'd been talking to some of the other bosses and they thought he'd been too hard on me. He then said that my mother had called him and he thought she was about to divorce him. She'd threatened to put a 'For Sale' sign in the front yard of the house if he didn't give me my job back. He told me I could start back right away. I said I'd start back tomorrow.

I had got a job on a mine site where Dave was the mine manager at seventeen, and he got me the job. I was a dump truck driver and it was tough. He threw me into one of these dump trucks, which I'd never driven. They call it 'hot seat training'. Nowadays you have to spend about sixty to eighty hours in the passenger seat of a dump truck and get trained properly before you can start driving one. It was a hard mine to drive at because it's all clay and mineral sands, and they always used to say if you can drive a dump truck there you can drive a dump truck anywhere. It's boggy and clayey and often raining, and dump trucks are spinning sideways in the clay. It's treacherous. So, Dave just threw me in a truck with somebody and I was in there for the day and then an LV (light vehicle) came down and the woman in the truck got out, and I was left sitting there. Then the boss called me and asked me what I was doing. I told him I was waiting for someone to jump in the driver's seat, and he said, no, I was to hop in and drive it. I couldn't believe it! It was a nightmare. And that's how I learned to drive a dump truck. In fact, I returned there twenty-odd years later and worked there again.

I met K's father there. His father owned a couple of hardware shops and a couple of planes, so he was quite wealthy. He was an aerial photographer for BHP, the big mining company. K's father was well known around town and one day he walked up to me when I was washing my hands at a big basin. He said, 'What are you doing down here?' I replied, 'What are *you* doing down here?' I'd seen him around at parties and the pub and various places. He then gave me a lift into town. That was the beginning. To me he was the best thing since sliced bread. I'd had brief encounters with other guys but nothing like this, this was serious. I wondered what he saw in me. I felt I was lucky, although now I think it was he who was lucky. I look at K now and see his father, he's a one hundred per cent clone of his father: the way he walks, the way he looks, everything. It's nice to see this resemblance. My mother commented that K shines, he has since he was little, but he doesn't get it – he thinks people are looking at his girlfriend but they're looking at him. He's an extremely attractive person but he's totally unaware of it.

About six months after I met K's father, he said he was going to Europe. He'd been planning this trip since before I met him. It was to be a holiday. He asked me to come with him, but I had to wait until I turned eighteen and then I flew to England and met him over there. We travelled around Europe together for about six months. We went to Germany for the Oktoberfest, I got a job in a pub in England, we went to Italy and Greece. We met some interesting people along the way. It was a new world for me – I'd never travelled overseas before. It was a happy time. I remember travelling from England to France in a hovercraft and not even having to go through customs, we just travelled straight to Paris, but when we went to Spain they pulled us over because we hadn't had our passport stamped when we entered France. We went to Amsterdam and smoked some pot. For a girl from Newman, it blew my mind. Europe was a whole other world – I had no idea places like these existed. I was just a tiny dot in an ocean of people. I wanted to go to Africa but we ran out of money; we got as far as Barcelona. I have good memories of that trip, but at the end I was happy to come back to Australia.

We lived in Perth. K's father was working and I got pregnant. It was a bit of a surprise but it was nice, I was happy. I knew it was going to be a boy and I knew I was going to call him K. K's father was rapt, he wanted a boy too. He was a good dad. He thought K was the best thing ever. My brother Ross had a baby, Perrin, who's five months older. We ended up living in the same place and K and Perrin grew up as quite tight little cousins.

By the time K was born, we were living in Karratha. At the time, Dave was a boss in Dampier in Karratha and he offered K's father a job up there. After that we moved to Pannawonica in the Pilbara. It was a tiny town where K's father was working for a big mining company. I never wanted to get into mining. After school, all the other kids ended up working for BHP and I just thought, no, I'm not doing that, and then I ended up doing it anyway. I remember K saying the same thing, he was adamant. Now he's an apprentice up on a mine site.

Mining's a strange world. If you fly in and out it's like flying onto another planet – you find yourself out of touch with the rest of the world, doing twelve hour days, seven days a week, then seven night shifts. By the time you've travelled to and from the site, it's anything up to fourteen hours. You're tired all the time, and everything becomes a blur. You lose touch with reality and you don't know what's going on in the rest of the world. You're sort of living two lives, the one at home with your family, where you find suddenly your time there has gone, the week is over and it felt like two days, then you fly back to the mine and you might as well be on Mars. That's how it tears families apart. What happens a lot is that people working on the mines end up with an extra partner, then you see them getting off the plane at Perth airport and their wives or husbands and little children run into their arms and I'd just think: you piece of shit. And those women at home on their own sometimes branch out and make new friends, develop new interests, find new jobs, so when their husbands come home it's like being a stranger in your own home. It's like being a stranger in your own life.

We were living in Pannawonica. I'd been with K's father since I was seventeen and I'd had K when I was twenty-two. I loved K's father but I wasn't in love with him anymore. I wasn't ecstatic about our relationship and I sat on that for a while until one day I told him. It was one of the hardest things I've ever done and maybe it was a mistake, I'm not sure now. He was devastated. He wanted us to still live in the same house and sleep in separate rooms but I wasn't prepared to do that. We started fighting and arguing all the time. It was tough. He and my brother were close, my family loved him and he was a good father. It was a terrible time, an absolute disaster. I think the biggest problem was a lack of communication. We needed to talk more and he didn't want to. I'd see problems and he couldn't see that there were any. In the end, I just thought, no, I'm not doing this for the rest of my life. His dad died two days after I told him it was over and they were close, so it was a big kick in the gut for K's father. His life fell to pieces; it was a shitty time. I felt cruel. I thought maybe I should stay with him because it just devastated me, I felt completely gutted.

When K's father and I broke up the only things we argued about were the Jim Beam fridge and Thai, the dog.

And then of course there was K. I felt that I was taking K away from his father, which I didn't want to do because they were very close. I kept asking myself: what am I doing? I'm just going to screw this up big time. I had my mother, my brother, all my family on my back about it. Now when I think about it and all the troubles I've had in my life, I kick myself. I think maybe, when I thought my life was so shithouse, it wasn't really. It probably could have been fixed and I'll always regret it. He wanted me to go back to him even years later, and I wanted to, but I was just too stubborn. I did want to go back, and now I'm crying just thinking about it. I haven't been with him since K was four and it still hurts so much. I now think it was a huge mistake. I was young and stupid and didn't think it through properly. Now I look at other people's relationships and think, no, there was nothing wrong with mine, maybe it was all in my head. I hadn't seen him for quite a long time and then I saw him at K's eighteenth birthday and he still had that same look, a way of looking. And K told me not that long ago, 'Dad was crying in the shed the other day.' I said, 'About what?' He said, 'About you.' It still hurts so much. Why did I do that?

I stayed in Pannawonica for a while and K's father used to come around and pick K up all the time and one day he said, 'You're going to take K away, aren't you?' I said, 'No, you can see K whenever you want to, you don't have to ask, you can come and take him out whenever you want to. I'm not taking him away from you, I'm taking me away from you.' So he would pick K up and even if K and I had something planned, if his father wanted to see him I'd always let him have him. Even later when he was in boarding school, K used to fly up every school holidays and stay with his dad. There were never any restrictions on access. My feeling was always: he's not mine, he's ours, it's not my right to deny access. I'd never do that and I've never said a bad word to K about his father. I always wanted K to think highly of his father. Whenever K and I have spoken about the breakup I've just told him that we didn't get on. They often used to go out camping or fishing or whatever they used to do. There was never any bad feeling over money.

He eventually met another woman, maybe when K was about fourteen. She treats him well and seems to think well of him.

I came home from Newman one day in 2004 when I was working up there on a two and two roster. I went down to see my parents. They were talking about the Boxing Day tsunami that had just happened. I had no idea. I'd heard no radio, I might as well have been mining on the moon and it doesn't matter to you because you're either mining or you're at work. The Christmases I worked when K was at boarding school, I missed K's year twelve graduation, I missed his birthday parties, I missed little things that may not seem like much but I knew that they meant so much. And you can't do anything about it unless you quit your job – which I've done in the past just so somebody could be there for him, whereas his father never did because he knew I was going to.

CHAPTER SEVEN

BEVAN

I was twenty-six when I left K's father. It was difficult being in that situation, living in a small town where everyone knew everyone. K's father was supporting us financially and I could continue living in the mine house. Ross was living around the corner from me so I was lucky. At the same time I was a bit lost. The rest of my family was nineteen hundred kilometres away, which was hard. I had lots of friends, but I missed Mum and the rest of the family as there was only Ross and me.

Socially there was a lot of drinking as there always is on mines. And there were barbecues, going out to the river and swimming, camping and fishing. After Amsterdam, I never touched drugs again (apart from that one time in prison later), and I didn't want C around people who did, so I gave up quite a few friends as a result. And I guess it worked – K never got into drugs. He enjoys a drink but not excessively. K is one thing I never regretted; I've always been so happy to be his mum. He was always content as a child and still is a very cruisy, happy person.

I went back to work when I met Bevan. After K's father's dad died, Bevan started coming around to see if I was OK. I was still twenty-six at the time. I knew him in Pannawonica. He worked at the mine and worked with Ross. I was with him from when K was five until he turned eight. I was quite devastated about the breakup with K's father and I wasn't very impressed with Bevan or his visits. There were only a couple of hundred people in the town and you knew everybody. I thought he was a nice enough bloke, good-looking, funny, eleven years older than me. He also got along well with K, but my mum and my brother didn't like him. My mother never explained why but Ross said he had this horrible look about him and I couldn't see it. It was a year or so before we started a relationship. He'd started coming around to see if I was OK, then he started doing things around the house and helping. K's father, meanwhile, got another company house in town and the mine told him that I couldn't stay in the mine house any longer, so Bevan moved in so I could keep the house. We'd started a relationship a couple of months before that. He was good to K and to me and we spent a lot of time going out camping and fishing and so on.

But I started to notice that he didn't like me spending time with my friends and I was aware that something wasn't right there. I think this was an early sign of his jealousy. He'd get angry if a girlfriend dropped in wanting me to go over to her place, or go out to the river with K and her kids. I was happy being with him in the beginning, so I suppose I pushed my friends away. It was strange that in this small town I hadn't heard anything bad about him, but now looking back on it there was a lot of stuff I didn't know. I didn't know why he'd broken up with his ex-partner. He just said she left him.

Then things changed and I saw a person I didn't know. He became cruel and started punching me. The first time it happened we were washing his big boat and he told me to squirt the hose on some area but I didn't do it right. God forbid that I didn't know how to squirt some car or a boat! He tried to jam the hose connection in my mouth, forcing it open and making it bleed. I didn't know what the hell was going on and I took off to the bedroom. He came in and picked me up and threw me against the wall, breaking the fibreboard. I was in shock. I'd never experienced anything like that before. I was so scared. He was a big bloke, well over six foot, and I was fifty-two kilos. He told me I was a fucking idiot and, 'Do what I tell you to do!'

And then the apologies came, 'I'm sorry, I've never done anything like that before and I won't ever do it again and I promise and I don't know what happened, I just lost my temper.'

knew nothing about this side of him. No-one had told anything. I believed that he wouldn't do it again, but believed that he'd done it before. Looking at the 'd done it, it all came very easily to him. And yet ad been no warning – he'd never been angry with re, he'd never shouted at me, he suddenly just . I told no-one about this, not even my brother. I as too scared to, although there and then I knew to leave. But K's father was still in Pannawonica 't want to take K away from him, I still wanted K ther.

as big and muscular and strong. He used to be a c before he worked at the mine site. After that ever thing settled down for a while, but he'd do little ike push me or yell at me a lot. He'd smack me ar er something trivial like not having dinner ready, do it while K was in the bath. Then when K came ou be nice; it was like nothing had happened. K never ything. Gradually the abuse got worse. He would use ts and he never worried where he hit me. He'd drag ound by my hair, hit me in the mouth or the stomach they were hard hits, big thumps. Other triggers were nds visiting, or when K's father came to pick up K and be nice to him, then after he'd left Bevan wouldn't talk to , or he'd shut me out of my bedroom or lock me out of t ouse so I'd sit outside all day.

After we'd moved down to Bridgetown, we went out for dinner and drinks at the local pub one night with one of his workmates and his wife. I was standing at the bar and Bevan came over and told me we were going home. I told him I wasn't going home. It was school holidays and K was with his dad and I decided I was going to take a taxi to my mother's place. She was also living in Bridgetown at the time. So he walked out of the pub, but then he turned around and stormed back in and grabbed me by the hair and dragged me out through the doors and towards the car. As he tried pushing me in through the passenger door, I made a break for it and ran. I hid down near some shops and he couldn't find me so he went home. I decided I wouldn't go to my mum's house because I didn't want her to know what was going on, I didn't want her to be worrying about me. I caught a taxi home and the lights in the house were all out. I opened the glass sliding doors and he was hiding behind the curtains there. He started laying into me and then threw me through the door. I would have called someone but he'd cut the phone lines again.

Bevan broke two of my ribs and my nose and I don't think I break very easily. He'd hurt me until I cried, but after a while I didn't cry anymore. The next morning my mum and sister arrived. Mum took one look at me and burst into tears. My sister said, 'I'm going to kill him!' and she went down the hallway to the bedroom and he started shoving her around and shouting abuse at her. He pushed her out the door and told her to fuck off, 'This isn't your fuckin' house!' My mum said to me, 'Have you seen yourself in the mirror?' I hadn't.

It must have been soul destroying for her because he used to give me a bloody nose, split eyes and pull my hair out. He'd often strangle me, choking me. He also used to bite me. Once he bit me on the nose and told everyone the puppy had done it. Once he bit a piece out of my calf, on my shin bone. I've got a scar about ten centimetres long on the top of my head where he smashed a bottle over it. And he'd suffocate me with pillows. We had a pool and sometimes he would try and drown me in it. He'd do these things when K was at his father's place for holidays.

One time I went to my mum's place and she rang the police and told them he had an unlicensed firearm in the back of his car. They asked what kind of car he had and they pulled him up and they apparently didn't find anything. He said to me, 'Ha, they found the firearm in the car and they didn't do anything about it. You're fucked now, aren't you?' So, I don't know what was going on because every time I made a complaint or signed a restraining order, it got me in worse trouble because he'd then know I'd done it, and the cops weren't following up or doing what they were supposed to be doing.

He also used to attack me in the shops. We might be in Coles after we'd moved up to Port Hedland, and he'd just stop in an aisle and look at me, then punch me in the face in front of everyone. He didn't care who saw him. After that he got worse and he'd hit me in public often. When he hit me in public, people would sometimes step in and try to stop him, but he was so verbally abusive and aggressive that they were too scared to do anything.

I used to have to go to hospital although he would never take me there. The day after he threw me through the glass door I had to go to hospital for stitches to a big gash under my chin. They stitched me up and the woman doing it asked what had happened. I told her I'd fallen over and she looked at me strangely. Then Bevan walked in and she said, 'I reckon he did that to you,' and I said, 'No, he didn't.' Bevan said, 'Yes, I did do that to her and she fuckin' deserved it.' He didn't care, he had no shame. It was embarrassing.

I remember the first time I met Bevan's brother, Larry, in Port Hedland, he looked at me and he looked at Bevan and he said, 'You've been hitting her, aye?' He said, 'What?' His brother repeated his question and added, 'It looks like her nose has been broken.' Bevan said, 'Nah,' and his brother said, 'You have. Do you remember what it was like when we were all younger, Bevan, and Dad used to do that to Mum?' I got to know Bevan's brother quite well. He told me that he doesn't have a girlfriend because he does it to his women too. The two brothers had frequent arguments about what he was doing to me and he'd tell him he had to stop. He told me one day, 'We used to call Bevan the caveman because he likes to drag his women around by the hair.' He said, 'He'll kill you. One of you is going to die.' And he was right. Bevan had no respect for my family or anyone, he just didn't care.

My sister Helen came up there with her partner Scott for a couple of days and we went fishing. Scott had never met Bevan before and we went fishing out in the dinghy for the day. This is Helen's account of that day, which is close to my memory of it:

> Up at Hedland we'd been fishing; I don't know what time it was when we came in, it was the days before mobile phones, but the moon was right up. We got back in and Bevan grunted at Annette, which was the only way he ever spoke, 'Stop at the shop.' I didn't talk to him the whole time we were there. Annette pulled up at the shop and he was in the front passenger's seat. Annette was driving because he didn't have a licence, and I was sitting behind Bevan in the back. Bevan said, 'I haven't got any fucking money,' and Annette said, 'Why didn't you tell me and I would have stopped at the bank.' He just clouted her, gave her a backhander, and then everything went pear-shaped and I sat forward in between the seats because it was the HiLux, and I said, 'Stop hitting my sister!' He said, 'If you're not

careful, I'll hit you.' I said, 'You want to hit me? Hit me, I don't even care, I'll go to the cops.'

By that time Annette was screaming, 'Get out! Get out! Get out!' Scott got out of the car and next thing Bevan was getting out and I just lay down on the back seat. So, both men were outside but Scott wasn't ready and Bevan punched him and he hit the ground. Bevan then started to open the door to come and get at me, and at that moment I kicked the door open and it hit him. He swore at me and shoved the door back at me and I kicked it again and it hit him a second time and he pulled the door open and he was in the back of the car after me and I just kept on kicking to get him away and finally he just took off running like a scared rabbit.

We were back at the house when Bevan came walking down the front pathway. I said that was it, 'I'm boiling the kettle and if he comes anywhere near he's going to wear it.' The door was open so Scott got up and slammed the door shut and Bevan just took an axe to the hinges of the door and broke it down. I called the cops and they didn't care, by the time they got there I was probably a little bit rude and I didn't realise that one was the sergeant and I said, 'Where the hell have you bastards been?' because they hadn't shown up I told them exactly where we were and they just couldn't be bothered. It took them about three hours to get there.

Basically, he wanted Annette away from her family because we were a hindrance to what he was doing.

The police came around to me one day because Bevan had been hitting me and had kicked me in the face. One of the officers was Ron Billets. They tried to put Bevan in the back of the paddy wagon and in the process Bevan broke one of Ron's fingers. I remember it clearly. They took him to the police station, then they rang me up and said, 'We had to take him up to the Port Hedland Hospital to sedate him because we just couldn't deal with him.' They said, 'You can go home now.' I said, 'But he'll leave,' and they said, 'No, he won't leave, you don't have to worry about that.' I went to a friend's place just across the road from us and I watched Bevan come home. He smashed the back door in and I ended up going down to the police station. When I went in, they said that I looked terrified. I said, 'I'm terrified of him. Wherever I go, he comes.' They said, 'Well you don't have to worry, he won't come here,' and in walks Bevan. A fight broke out between Bevan and two coppers. In court, they said that wasn't true, but my lawyer had gone right back and found documentation on it. Why wasn't Bevan ever charged with any of that?

Any paperwork or documents the cops had on Bevan were lost. I'd taken out between ten and fifteen DVOs (domestic violence orders) against Bevan over the years and all the paperwork was lost. He assaulted Helen's boyfriend Scott. When we went home, Helen locked the door and when Bevan arrived home he put an axe straight through the hinges of the door, which cut it right off, and that's how he got into the house. Any papers or documents against him? Lost, including illegal possession of a sawn-off shotgun with a silencer and one hundred and fourteen rounds of ammo. Driving around without a licence – they'd pull him up and let him go every time.

One time I was inside with Bevan when the police came around because the neighbours had called them. He'd bitten a big chunk out of my face. The police were asking me to come outside and Bevan was seething, 'Go out there and I'll fucking kill you.' I told them I couldn't come out, but eventually I did and Bevan stayed inside. They said, 'If you sign this piece of paper, we'll put him in the lock-up and we'll send him to Perth. He'll go to jail; we've had it with him.' I refused to sign it. I told them it would just make it worse. I knew he'd be back to kick my head in. I remember it quite vividly because there was this one copper there, I'd never seen him before, he was from Perth or somewhere. Bevan was still inside and this copper was saying, 'Bevan are you going to come out here?' Bevan was going on, 'Go fuck yourselves,' and so on. I said, 'If I sign that, he's not coming back here?' They said, 'No.' I said, 'I've done this so many times before, it makes it worse, I'm telling you.' 'Sign it and he's going to be gone.'

Bevan came out and there was a big scene going on, he was yelling and screaming at me, they put him in the paddy wagon and they took him to the South Hedland lock-up. I actually rang them to make sure he was there and they said, 'Yeah, we're watching him through the cameras, he's here. He's going to be going to Perth tomorrow.' I thought, thank God for that, someone finally listens. Seven o'clock the next morning, Bevan's at the front door. I rang them up. I said, 'You said he wasn't going to be here.' They said, 'We didn't have anything to keep him on.' And they kept doing it. Did they want him to kill me or something? If they'd done their job to begin with, none of this would have happened. I still don't understand it. It was a nightmare.

Every time I took a DVO out against Bevan, he'd come around, the police would take him away and put him in the lock-up, then they'd let him go again and I'd find him back at my place. There was never any explanation from Bevan, it was always, 'Bad luck.' Bevan had this 'bad luck' thing going on, it was a common expression of his. There was a smugness there. DVOs don't just get cancelled. And sometimes it's not up to you, sometimes the police will put a twenty-four-hour restraining order on the offender so he's not allowed near the house for that period.

I can't be sure of the exact number and I can't check it because when the Port Hedland station closed and everything was moved to South Hedland police station, they say they lost all the paperwork during the transition. I'm sure there were computers then that would have all these incidents entered into the system. They also said they'd lost the record of the time he assaulted my sister and her boyfriend. He was never charged with anything and he never went to court for anything, not even the time he assaulted the cop in the Port Hedland police station. They denied it happened but it happened, I was there.

I was in Port Hedland for about three years. Some of these were court issues because I'd have to go to the Magistrates Court in Port Hedland where the restraining order would be put on him and he'd stay away for a little bit and then he'd just roll up, or I'd come home and he'd be in the house. I'd become nervy and jumpy because I never knew whether he'd be in the house. I'd always be looking over my shoulder because I didn't know where he was. I couldn't sleep properly because I'd hear a noise and I'd think it was him breaking into the house.

It was a vicious circle. He'd do something, I'd call the police or the neighbours would, they'd come around and there'd be a big discussion led by the police saying someone had to leave, he should leave, no maybe you should leave, I'd say I had nowhere to go whereas he could go to his brother, and I'd be sitting there all smashed up in the middle of all this destruction, and they'd always take his side. I couldn't understand it and it's hard to explain. And if they did make him leave and put a restraining order on him, he'd soon be back there again.

By 2002 it had got so bad that I finally told him I didn't want to be with him anymore, 'I just can't do it, I hate you, I hate what you represent.' He said, 'If I can't have you, no-one's going to have you.' There was nowhere to hide, he'd always find me and just roll up there. A lot of people feared him.

Sometimes I'd just run out the door and he'd chase me down the street. When he'd attack, he used to lock the doors and spend a couple of hours just doing stuff to me. Always this was when K was at his dad's.

Once I had to go down to Karratha to pick K up from his father's, which was a two hundred kilometre drive each way. Bevan came with me and for two hours he abused me, pulling my hair out, ripping my clothes. I thought I was going to die. In the end, he fell asleep and I got out of the car and I ran down the road to a friend's place at about five o'clock in the morning. I had no shoes on and he dragged me through the bush. I wanted to die. I got to my friend's place and Bevan had taken off with my car. I called the police and told them he'd stolen it. They told me that because we were de facto, they didn't class it as stealing even though it was in my name.

When I knocked on my friend's door, I still remember the look on his face. He said, 'What the fuck has happened to you?' I went inside and his wife came out and said, 'No way! You need to go to hospital.' I was a wreck and I said, 'I need you to call up K's father because he's dropping K off.' My friend said, 'Well, he's not seeing you like that!' When K's father arrived, he left K in the car for five minutes. K didn't know I was there. When K's father came in and saw me, he said, 'I'm going to fucking kill him, no fucking way!' And he just started yelling. He said he'd take K back home with him. It was school holidays so he had him for another two weeks. I then went up to the hospital and they couldn't believe the state I was in. The police were called in and they took a statement and photos and nothing ever happened.

I managed to get home because all my and K's stuff was still there. I walked through the door and Bevan was there. He said, 'Fuck me, what happened to you?' as if he had no idea. I couldn't keep him out of my house, if he wanted to get to me, he would.

I was dropping K at school one day and he had hopped out the back over the back seats. Just before I got out of the car, Bevan smashed me in the face. Then I had to pretend nothing had happened and had to walk K up to his class. And all this time I was trying to protect K from seeing any of it.

We went to a waterhole once, we had K and his little mate Peter with us. The boys were riding motorbikes and would have been seven. They were racing motocross then. Bevan was drinking beer out of those big king brown bottles. He smashed me on the head with a full one. I've got a big scar that runs right along my forehead underneath my hairline. In the cartoons, they say you see stars. I never believed that but I do now, I saw stars that day. My head had this massive gash in it and needed twenty-three stitches. I was staggering around when K came back on his motorbike. He asked, 'What happened?' There was just so much blood. I went down to the water to try and wash my face. The tailgate of my ute was down and I told him I'd thrown a stick for the dog and I smashed my head on the back tailgate. K just looked at me. Much later in court he was asked what he thought of Bevan and he said he didn't like him because he used to 'hit my mother. He used to hit my mum all the time.' So, he knew. I used to try and hide it from K all the time but you can't.

I told Bevan I needed to go to the hospital which was thirty kilometres away. He said, 'Well, you'll have to drive yourself.' I loaded the bikes up and he wouldn't let me go to the hospital so we went home. I told him he'd have to take K's little friend home and he refused and said I'd have to do it. I said, 'I can't go to his place like this, I've got to go to hospital.' He said, 'Well you're gonna have to.' So I tried to clean my face up but I couldn't stop it from bleeding. So

I held something on it and when I dropped Peter off, his dad said, 'What happened to you?' I told him I'd hit my head on the tailgate. He said, 'That fucking arsehole, you need to get away from him. You seriously need to get away from him.' I had to take K to school the next morning, and then I went to the hospital. They said, 'This should have been stitched yesterday. What happened?' I said, 'I hit my head on the tailgate.' They said, 'No you didn't, you've got glass in your head.' Bevan didn't care, it was a case of 'tough luck' and he didn't say that he didn't do it. He was quite open about the fact that he'd done it. He never tried to hide the fact that he'd done any of it. And because whenever he was arrested, he got off, he never paid the price. Although he did in the end.

I think I stayed with him because I think maybe I thought I loved him. Maybe I thought that it was going to get better. I don't know why. The truth is I don't have an answer for that. I think I felt sorry for him. He used to make me feel sorry for him. 'I'm gonna get help, I'm gonna get better, I don't want to lose you, it's not your fault, it's me, I'm gonna see somebody about it, I don't want to be alone, I couldn't live without you,' and on and on. They play on your softest part and you think, oh well, maybe if he gets help... But it's just a load of shit, they're talking rubbish to you. And I suppose because I was alone and had no family around me, I don't know, he just made me feel sorry for him, I guess.

I stayed with him a while longer and then my mum said she was coming up and I asked her not to, I knew it would just make things worse. She came anyway and stayed in a hotel. Whenever she came over, Bevan would totally ignore her, wouldn't say a word to her. K spent some time with her, then she begged me to come home with her, and I said, 'I can't, I just can't.'

So, she went home and a couple of days after that I said to him, 'I'm leaving and I don't care what you do to me because I'm leaving. I don't want to do this anymore, this is fucked.' Then he started crying and saying, 'You're taking my family away.' I replied, 'I'm not taking your family away, I'm taking my son and myself away from you,' and then he started threatening me, telling me what he was going to do to me, 'I'll kill you. I'll go down and kill your mum.' I said, 'I don't give a fuck, I'm leaving.'

I rang up K's father and asked if I could come and stay for a while and he said, 'Yep, yep, yep, yep, yep, yep, yep.' I threw as much stuff as I could fit in the car, put K in and went to his father's. Bevan cried and asked what he was going to do now. I said I don't know.

CHAPTER EIGHT

A New Beginning?

I was in Pannawonica with Mum for about a week and then he started ringing. 'I'm really sorry, I've changed, come back. I'm going to counselling now. I'm gonna stop drinking.' On and on.

And I went back to him.

CHAPTER NINE

BJ

One of BJ's neighbours described him as a great neighbour, a nice guy, someone who was known for doing things for people, especially those who couldn't pay with anything but friendship and thanks. She said people loved him as he was a character who was always happy and cheery. He would always be working on cars and bikes, and she remembered that one time he fixed up a four-wheeler bike for a boy whose father was very ill and wasn't able to. It was just the sort of kind thing he would do. He was also an inventor and the neighbour recounted he made a motorised scooter by taking a whipper snipper apart and then went zipping around town. That was the first one anyone had seen.

The neighbour also described him as so conscientious. During her house renovation, she inadvertently took out a support beam, which was bad because her husband was away. BJ had come straight round and welded a new one in that afternoon. It was precision work and he was spot on.

I knew BJ well; he was a lot older than me and was a friendly bloke. He got on well with people but he didn't like Bevan. He was a pretty good friend, he was a mate, someone we'd go around to for a barbecue. I never asked him about his personal life. He was very placid; he was a good person.

He had chickens and rabbits and he was building a big house. He used to wear sarongs and stuff, he was sort of like a little old hippy and everyone called him BJ. He was about fifty-four, maybe twenty-five years older than me. He was a bit like a father figure to me in a way. K's father knew him, he had a big workshop and used to fix people's motorbikes and cars.

I first met BJ when Bevan was working for local concreter. They used to keep a lot of their work equipment up at BJ's house, and one day I got a phone call from Bevan asking me to go up to this address to pick him up after work, and that's when I was introduced to BJ.

It was one of those places where a lot of kids used to go to. It was just nice being there. K used to go up there and BJ would say, 'Hello, little man,' and he used to make K swords and stuff. K liked him. BJ had a big workshop that he was living in while he was building his house and he had a lot of stuff there that little kids used to like looking at, like old army stuff or little trinkety things. He had chickens and he had a dog and he had big aviaries down the side of his house, and he lived right on the beach so the kids used to go down to the beach from there.

He was kind and gentle, he never argued or got into trouble or fights. He wasn't impressed with what Bevan was doing to me, he couldn't believe it. He used to call me 'Trouble', in an affectionate way, 'Hello, Trouble,' or 'Here comes Trouble.' My mum went to visit him when he was in jail. I asked her why and she said, 'Just to see what he's like.' She said, 'I was waiting there in the visiting room and I was expecting this big, massive man to come out, then this tiny bloke came out and said, "Hello, you must be Annette's mum," and there he was, quietly spoken, polite, well-mannered.' I asked Mum what she'd expected and she didn't know, but someone big.

During the motocross season, we would maybe go once a week, maybe once a fortnight, to BJ's, depending on when the bike needed some work done. He fixed the starter motor in my car; he fixed the starter motor in Bevan's ute; he was making up another back step for the back of my HiLux after someone had run into the back of it. He used to make things for K, fix K's pushbikes, just help people out. He didn't only do this with me, he did it for many people.

A couple of times there were issues about Bevan keeping some of his work stuff there. I'm not too sure what it was about, I just know they had a falling-out. This lasted for months. I didn't see BJ maybe for six months one time, and then at one stage I didn't see him for about a year. That was probably after the time Bevan made a comment about someone else and said something like, 'That bloke should sort her out by giving her a thumping,' and BJ said, 'Only a gutless coward would do that.' Bevan punched BJ on the face and BJ landed on the floor. It wasn't the only time Bevan went for BJ but it was the only time he did any real damage. It took BJ quite a while to pull himself up off the floor and he was seeing stars. There was no contact between them for a long time after that, BJ apparently asked Bevan's boss not to bring him around anymore, but eventually Bevan went back when he needed his ute or K's motorbike fixed, and BJ was too nice to say no.

I thought of BJ like a brother, I suppose, a friend, a mate. If I saw him after Bevan had given me a beating, he would ask me what had happened and I would say just about the same thing, 'Bevan did it.' I didn't go into fine detail about what had happened. It got to the stage where he'd say, 'What's happened?' and I'd say, 'You don't really need to ask, do you?' and he'd sort of say, 'No, not really.' There wasn't very much discussion about it because he already knew.

Bevan used to drink three or four cartons of VB stubbies a week easily. If we went out to the motocross, he'd drink a whole carton, and K used to train Mondays, Wednesdays and Fridays, and he would race on some weekends.

One Friday, K finished school and we went out to the motocross track and he was practising on his bike. He fell off and broke the throttle and it was all jammed full of sand. This happened late in the afternoon around five thirty or six o'clock, so we went up to BJ's place, me, Bevan and K with the bike in the back. BJ came out and took the throttle off K's bike and cleaned it out and said that we could pick it up on the Sunday.

On the Sunday, I got up around nine thirty. K was up watching a movie. He was always an early riser and would be up and about at five thirty to six o'clock every morning without fail. It was a lazy day. I got K some breakfast, then I mucked around with him out the front. He was bouncing up and down on the trampoline and the dog was on there with him, and we were throwing a frisbee around in the backyard. It was a hot day.

Two days earlier we'd heard something about a cyclone, a blue code. It means that a cyclone is brewing if it's blue alert, and when it's getting a little bit worse it's yellow, and then you've got red alert, which means you're not allowed outside. We had gone around to Bevan's brother's place and helped him prepare, filled his dinghy full of water and stuff like that, tied some things down, and had then gone home. Bevan had thrown some rope over the carport to hold our carport down in case tin flew everywhere, and he filled the dinghy up with water so it couldn't be blown away. That's the standard routine up there during storm season.

Bevan got up about midday and later K wanted to go across the road to play with a friend but Bevan didn't want him to, he wanted to go to his brother's place. Neither K nor I wanted to go. We got to Larry's in the late afternoon, maybe five o'clock. On the way, we stopped at the drive-through bottle shop as Bevan wanted to get a carton of VB. We went in Bevan's white ute because my red HiLux was still at BJ's waiting for the back step to be fixed. It was just a ute that we bought especially for putting K's bike in the back because as K's bikes got bigger, they became too big for the back of the HiLux.

When we got to Larry's, he and one of his mates were watching the cricket. We stayed a couple of hours until K said he was tired and bored and wanted to go home. I was tired and wanted to go home too and Matt told Bevan he should also leave, as there was another three hours of cricket left and Bevan didn't even like cricket. Bevan had drunk over half a carton easily. It was about seven o'clock, I'd had a couple of ciders and was ready for home and to get K fed and into bed. When we got outside, Bevan said he wanted to go to BJ's to pick up K's throttle for his motorbike. Again, neither K nor I wanted to go but we went anyway.

Bevan drove and I was sitting in between him and K. We had an argument on the way and Bevan smacked me in the nose. It started bleeding and I ended up with blood on my polo shirt and cut-off denim shorts. We got to BJ's sometime after seven o'clock and we sat around his pool table which he also uses as a kitchen table. We were having a few drinks and I decided that K should have something to eat so we ordered some Chinese food.

Outside, Bevan and I argued about who was going to go and pick the food up. He was drunk and he didn't have a licence, and I didn't want him being picked up by the police. He verbally abused me, just the usual, said I was a fucking arsehole, that I don't do as I'm told, I'm a piece of shit, I was a cunt, and so on. I just said, 'OK, whatever then.' He drove down and picked up the food.

By the time he got back, K was ratty and tired and was asking to go home. We all sat down and ate the Chinese and Bevan carried on drinking. After we had finished the meal, I said I wanted to go home, but again Bevan didn't want to so we ended up having another argument. I more or less said, 'Well, I'm going to take K home and I'm going to take my car then.' BJ tried to calm things down and offered to get my car out saying it was OK to drive. He said, 'Annette, you can take the boy home and Bevan and I will stay, he can stay a bit longer.' This only made things worse. Bevan got angry with BJ and told him to butt out. Then he said, 'You can take the fucking thing then, I'm going!' and he stormed out and hopped in his car, angry and drunk. He could consume a lot of alcohol without becoming staggeringly blind drunk. We heard the wheels spin on the gravel as he took off in a stink. That was the night he died.

I sat at the table for a little bit while K finished a drink, and BJ opened the roller doors and took my car out of the workshop. K jumped in the car and I spoke to BJ for maybe ten or fifteen minutes more while K was just lying down on the back seat of the car. As soon as he hopped in there, he would usually lie down and go to sleep.

BJ and I talked about Bevan's state of mind. I was scared to go home. We talked about how he would be when I got home, and I was worried about taking K there because I knew that there was going to be trouble. I told BJ I had to go because the consequences when I got home would be worse the longer I stayed.

He said that he wanted to come around to make sure that K and I were alright and I told him that I didn't think it was a very good idea. He was only little, like me, but he wanted to come and I more or less said OK. He said he would go around there and have a few beers with Bevan, maybe have a talk with him to settle him down. He could do that at times, take Bevan's mind off an argument. I still didn't think it was a very good idea but I agreed to it.

BJ said he'd follow us home so I hopped in my car and drove away with K asleep in the back seat and his dog in the back of the car. When I pulled up in the driveway, I could see lights on in the house and when I turned the engine off, I could hear music coming out from the open door.

CHAPTER TEN

Fateful Night

I expected that I'd probably find Bevan in K's bedroom, lying down on the carpet listening to music. He sometimes did that when he was drunk. K had a big stereo in his bedroom that his father had given him.

BJ's lights were behind me at one stage on the way home, but when I turned into my driveway, I couldn't see his car anywhere. I waited a little while and then I rang him to see where he was. He had parked around the corner because he was worried about Bevan damaging his car which he had just spent years restoring. I met him walking towards me up the street and together we walked towards the house.

I wanted to see where Bevan was so I could put K to bed. I didn't want to have a great huge argument which would wake K up, and I didn't want K to have to listen to another row or to hear Bevan beating me up. I didn't want trouble, I just wanted to put K to bed, or if not, put him on the lounge to sleep. Normally if Bevan had passed out on the floor in K's room, I would put K to sleep on the lounge or I would sometimes take him to bed with me, but Bevan hated K sleeping in our bed.

I went into the house first, BJ following behind. We were both scared, not knowing how we'd find Bevan. I found out in court that BJ spotted a fish filleting knife on a pot plant stand on the veranda just before he went in the door. He picked it up and put it in his pocket.

The front door was open and only the flyscreen door was closed. We could still hear the music coming from K's bedroom. We moved towards it and found Bevan lying asleep on his back on K's bedroom floor. I was standing behind BJ and I told him to get K's quilt from the bed so I could put him to sleep on the lounge. I warned him not to disturb Bevan. BJ stepped into the bedroom and I stayed standing outside K's bedroom door. I watched BJ step over Bevan to get the quilt and pillows. But just as he was stepping over him, Bevan woke up.

Bevan looked directly at me and at BJ. He growled at BJ, 'What the fuck are you doing in here?' By this time BJ was standing right over him, with one foot either side of him and one hand on the bed. Bevan had this look on his face that he gets when he's enraged, and it's just scary. It means that he's going to do something horrible; I've seen that look many times.

Straightaway Bevan pushed himself up with his left hand and threw a punch up at BJ with his right. I didn't know where it landed, all I could see was BJ's back, but it turned out he got BJ in the throat. His voice is probably still croaky to this day as a result, as it was in court two and a half years later. Bevan was shouting, 'What the fuck are you doing here? You fucking arsehole!' Bevan was half up by this time, crouching and ready to stand.

I took off. I went outside to the car where K was still asleep. I jumped in the car and I was going to leave because I didn't want K to wake up. I was scared at what was happening. I thought Bevan was going to bash BJ. I stayed in there for maybe a few minutes. It seemed like a long time but it couldn't have been. I could hear noises coming from the house, something that sounded like someone was jumping up and down on floorboards fighting. There were voices yelling. It just sounded like mumble to me but I could hear that it was BJ and Bevan's voices. I could hear the music still playing on the stereo.

After a few minutes, which felt like hours, I got out of the car. I wanted to see if BJ was alright, I was worried for him. I went to the front door but I didn't go in. By now I couldn't hear any noises coming from inside except the music. I went back to the car. I was standing by the back car door where I could see K asleep through the window. I stood there for maybe a couple of seconds and then I went into the house, not knowing what to expect, fearing the worst but hoping BJ was OK.

The bedroom door was still open. Bevan was lying face down on the floor and BJ was standing over the top of Bevan with his foot on K's T-ball bat across the back of Bevan's neck. The bat was held horizontally to the ground, on the back of his neck, and his right foot was applying pressure.

There was a lot of blood around Bevan's head and upper body, and all over the floor. I shouted, 'What have you done?' He turned to look at me. He said, 'He's dead. I've killed him,' and that he was sorry. He was crying. It was like the whole world just turned black. He said that once he started, he couldn't stop or he would have been killed, that Bevan just kept getting back up. He kept on saying he was sorry. I started yelling at him. I said that he was a fucking idiot and that he had killed Bevan and he'd done it in my son's bedroom and I wasn't very happy about that. I didn't think this could be happening. I felt sick, I couldn't think properly, I was stressed out, I was scared. I was having trouble getting words out. I was also crying. I think I was in a state of shock, I did not expect anything like this would happen. I thought there was just going to be a fight and that Bevan was going to beat BJ up. I did not want this to happen. This all took only seconds and BJ was starting to throw up. I pushed him towards the bathroom and he vomited in the toilet.

I could hear BJ vomiting in the bathroom. He wanted a drink to take the taste out of his mouth so I went and got him a beer out of the fridge. I don't know why beer; I just gave him a beer. We were both panic-stricken. I went outside to see if K was asleep still. I was horrified at the thought that he might wake up and come in and see all this mess. Then I went back inside.

I went into K's bedroom and I took the quilt cover off the quilt and his sheets off the bed and I threw them in the washing machine because I didn't want K to see his bedding like that if he came inside, I didn't want him to see any blood on his bed. The pillows and pillowcases didn't have blood on them so I took them and put them in the car. BJ had gone out and tried to wash off the blood on his arms and the bat with the water in the boat. He then went inside and used the laundry sink, and then started trying to clean up the bedroom floor and walls with a towel.

I had come back into the house after taking the pillows out and I'd changed my t-shirt because I'd decided I was going to take K to his father's place, and my shirt was all filthy from being up at BJ's workshop – K had been crawling all over me and there was blood on it from Bevan hitting me on the way to BJ's. I didn't want K's father to see any of that. I didn't wash the t-shirt; I just threw it on the bed.

I saw BJ cutting K's carpet up. I went out again to check on K. I was like a headless chook, I couldn't think straight, I didn't know what I was doing.

BJ had rolled Bevan's body up in the carpet that he had cut out. He was trying to drag him out of the bedroom. He asked me to help him but I said I couldn't touch him because it made me sick, what had happened. I couldn't go anywhere near him after that. I saw what he was doing but I kept on going out through the back door to see if K was alright.

BJ dragged Bevan outside, down the stairs and across the driveway into the carport, rolled up in the carpet.

I went back up to see if K was alright because my car was parked facing down into the driveway, down where Bevan's ute was. If he woke up, he would be able to see what was happening in the carport.

When I got back to the carport, BJ was about to start hoisting Bevan's body up onto the back of the ute. He told me that he'd tried lifting him but couldn't even get his shoulders off the ground. There was rope was there from when it was used to tie the patio down during the cyclone. He cut off a piece and fed it over a beam in the carport towards the back of the ute and put the rope around his torso and his shoulders, chest and whatever else, and lifted it up. He had coiled it over the rafter and under his foot with a loop, and every time he lifted him a bit, he could take the slack up under his foot. He would lift a bit, an inch or two, and take up the slack until he got him just over halfway up, till his waist was about the same height as his.

That's when he asked me if I could back the ute up for him because he now had him up to tailgate level but couldn't move anything from that height. I backed the ute right up until he could lower him down onto the ute.

I asked him what the hell we were going to do because it was all a fucking mess. He said that he was going to go and bury him out on a dirt track somewhere. At some stage BJ had asked me to call the ambulance or the police and I told him I wasn't doing any of that, I said, 'You did this, I've got K in the car.' K was my priority and I didn't want him around ambulances and police and everything that would go with that. In any event the police weren't phoned.

BJ said not to follow him, but I wouldn't take my son out to let him witness something like that, and plus you could never dig a hole up there because the ground is like concrete. I told him I was going to take K to his father's house in Pannawonica.

Everything just seemed like a blur. I couldn't think properly. I put the dog in the back of the ute. I didn't think about any provisions; I didn't know what to think. I was just doing things in a panicked daze. I thought that I could take K to his father's and drop him off, because if I took him to someone else's house I'd have to explain what had happened and I didn't want to. I never thought of what to do next. I didn't think that far ahead.

CHAPTER ELEVEN

Caught

Once in the car, all I wanted was to get out of there. I was anxious to get away as fast as I could. I was confused and panicky so I drove down to the beach for a while to get my head clear. Once I started driving again to take K to his dad's, I found BJ on the road ahead of me. I couldn't overtake him on Wilson Street which is the only way out of town and which sweeps around until it heads south, and then once it straightens out, there's a railway bridge which you can't pass on. I was planning to just keep on heading south from the intersection at the end of Wilson Street and that would take me all the way to Pannawonica. I didn't know where BJ was going but it turned out he was planning to turn left at the intersection and drive up the Great Northern Highway which heads north to Broome.

As I came over the bridge, I could see police lights up ahead, just south of the Wilson Street intersection. They looked like they were coming towards me so I quickly decided to turn left at the intersection where BJ had turned. I wasn't intentionally following BJ; I just took that turn to get away from the police. They were doing a routine patrol and had stopped someone to breathalyse them, and as they were walking back to their car, they saw our lights heading out of town, turning towards Broome.

I followed behind BJ for a while but he was going slow and after a while he indicated for me to overtake him. I found out later that the lights on the ute were getting dimmer and dimmer and he could hardly see anything once we were out of the lit zone, and my lights behind him were making things worse.

I drove past him and the cops came up behind him shortly after and followed him. I carried on for quite a while longer and then, not knowing what to do, I pulled into a dirt track on the left-hand side of the road. I needed to think about what was happening, try to make some sense of what was going on. I sat there for a bit and then I made a couple of phone calls. I phoned K's father first; his answering machine picked up and it did the next few times too. When my calls eventually woke him up, I told him that Bevan and I had had an argument and I didn't want to go home that night; I told him I was scared. I didn't tell him that Bevan had died, I needed to do that to his face. He told me just to come down to his place.

Then I rang my mother. I told her that BJ had killed Bevan. I said I didn't know what to do. I said I wanted to get to K's father, I wanted to take K to his father's place, and that I had no fuel in the car, and she said, 'Well, turn back.' I said I wanted to go back. I said, 'I'll have to go back,' and I said, 'I can't go to the house. I can't take K to the house.' I was rattled, very upset. Mum kept saying, 'You must get K to his father's. Get K to his father's.' 'I can't. I can't. I've got no fuel.' I just wanted to get to K's father's place. That was my plan. I said I'd call her later and I did, about an hour later, to say that I had turned back and the police were coming.

CHAPTER TWELVE

Snared

It seemed like I sat on that track off the side of the road for ages. Maybe it was half an hour, maybe twenty minutes, maybe an hour, I don't know, but eventually I turned around towards the police. I was still planning to get to K's father's place, but once I turned around, I knew the police were there, I could see their flashing lights coming towards me. You could see those lights a mile away in the black desert night.

After that first call to Mum, I'd tried to phone BJ a couple of times but it just rang out. I wanted to see if the police were down there because that's the way I had to go and I wanted to make sure that they weren't there. What I didn't know was that the cops had stopped BJ and discovered the body in the back. They were talking to him when his phone, which was lying on the seat of the ute, started ringing. They all looked at it and ignored it each of the three times I tried to call him.

The cop car was coming towards me, then it passed me, turned around and pulled me over. I was detained by the side of the road for hours. When they questioned me, I lied to them. I was hoping I could convince them that I thought Bevan was alive and at home so that they'd let me go on my way and I could get K to Pannawonica. I was scared. I was worried for my son. I didn't want him to find anything out. I didn't know when I was talking to them if he was listening. I didn't want him to hear any of it. I didn't believe that I'd done anything wrong.

I told them that Bevan and I had had an argument and I'd taken K out to the spoil bank and we'd sat there for a while and K hadn't wanted to go home. He'd fallen asleep and I said that I was taking him home now. The copper said that police had seen me overtake another vehicle about an hour before.

By that time, it was about three thirty in the morning. We then just made some small talk out on the highway about the dog and K and how he was the north-west champion for motocross.

He said in court that this small talk was just delaying tactics as they didn't want to take me back past the crime scene. They were waiting for some more information from the detectives who were there.

Eventually I said, 'What are we waiting out here for? It's getting cold.' He said, 'I'm just waiting for a couple of other police to tell us what's happening in town.' It was about a quarter past four by that time. I sat in the driver's seat of the car and the copper took the two phones away.

At daylight, I was taken back to the police station in Port Hedland.

CHAPTER THIRTEEN

Interrogation

They did a video interview with me and I told them a pack of lies. I should have just told them the whole sorry story but I'd never been in trouble before or in a situation like that. I still just wanted to get out of there and take K to his father's place, so I lied.

Initially, I was brought into an interview room where they started off friendly and chatty, like how are you, how are things going, how's your son? I wasn't offered a lawyer and I didn't think to ask for one because I wasn't under arrest or anything. Then it moved on to, 'We've got something to tell you, did you know Bevan is dead?' 'Expired' was the word they used. I started crying at that point. I was tired. I cared that Bevan was dead but I was worried about K – they had him there in another room and they're not allowed to do that. I kept asking for him and they'd say, no, he's alright, he's with a woman in another room. I told them I wanted someone to come and pick him up and they said they'd deal with that later. I got a bit cranky at that point. I insisted, 'No, I want someone to come and pick him up. I won't talk to you until we've arranged for someone to pick him up.' So, they let me call K's father to come and fetch him.

And then, 'We want you to know that we pulled [BJ] over and there was a body in the back of his ute.' I didn't think I was in trouble. I thought I'd just tell them what happened and they'd just let me go home. But soon I started thinking that this wasn't good. They changed, and they weren't so nice. They started to harden up and I wasn't having any of it. I didn't want to be there but didn't know that I didn't have to be. They wouldn't give me a phone call initially, but after a while they let me phone my mum. I told her where I was and I said, 'I'm not too sure but I think I'm in a bit of a world of shit.' There was no privacy – about six of them were standing there staring at me.

I'd been with police since between three and four in the morning and now it was about one o'clock in the afternoon. I'd had no sleep, I was tired and hungry. They'd given me something to drink but no food.

I remember one of the detectives. I didn't know him and he was nasty. The same questions kept coming and I said I didn't have to stay there, did I? They said they're advising me to, it's in my best interests. I felt very intimidated by them. I didn't even know whether it was daytime or night-time as they have fluorescent lights in there. They locked me up and then brought me out for interviewing five or six times. They'd come in and wake me up, they'd take me out, more questions, then take me back.

K's father arrived about lunchtime. He wasn't allowed to see me but he's quite loud and I could hear him. He said, 'I've come to pick my son up.'

'And you are?'

'I'm K's father, I want my son.'

'Well we might need to question you as well.'

'No, you're not, I've come here to pick my son up.'

'You need to wait and we need to talk to you.'

K's father got quite cranky and told them where to go.

'No, if you want to talk to me, I'll get a lawyer.'

And he grabbed K and left.

I had this feeling that they were going to question K and I didn't want K to know that Bevan had died. I didn't want him to know yet and I wanted to be the one to tell him.

After all this they took me up to the hospital. I wish I'd never gone. They told me I had to go up to get fingernail scrapings, hair samples and mouth swabs to gather DNA. I asked why, and they said I had to, and I thought, well, I've got nothing to hide. At the same time, I had a funny feeling that something was going on. When I got to the hospital, I asked the doctor if I had to do this and he said no, I didn't have to. I then looked at the coppers and said, 'I know what's going on here, I'm not stupid,' and that's when I started backing out of it, and after they'd taken the samples and we got back to the police station, I told them I wasn't going to talk to them anymore, I wanted to go. By then I had a strong feeling that I was going to get the blame for what BJ had done. I asked for another phone call, which they refused, saying that I'd already had one. They wouldn't let me phone a lawyer, telling me it was a public holiday. I said if they didn't give me another phone call, I wasn't talking to them anymore. This was maybe sometime before four o'clock in the afternoon. So, they let me have another phone call and I called my mum again.

When she answered, I told her that I needed a lawyer and she said she'd organised one and he was going to ring me soon. She asked me what was going on but the cops were almost standing on top of me and listening to every word I said. I told her I'd tell her later, but I was crying by now. I told her I didn't know what was going to happen and she started crying.

When I'd phoned her the night before on my way to K's father's and I told her what had happened, I'm not sure why, but I added, 'Please don't tell Dave.' I don't know why I said that except that I didn't want Dave to be disappointed in me. What a stupid thing to say, don't tell Dave.

I was still in the lock-up at four o'clock when my lawyer rang. This was my first lawyer who didn't get to represent me in court because they kept messing up the trial date and changing it. In the end the lawyer wasn't going to be available on the date they set so I had to get another one.

When he first spoke with me on the phone, with the police listening in, he introduced himself. He asked me where I was and I told him the South Hedland police station and he asked me if there were police standing there listening. I said yes, and he said he wanted me only to answer yes or no. He asked is there one? No. Are there three? No. Five? Yes. I don't want you to talk to them anymore. Have you been talking to them? Yes. Stop the conversation, tell them you want to leave the police station and that you're leaving right now. And that was it. I hung up and said, 'I want to leave.' They said, 'Well, you can't take the car.'

I wanted my stuff: my phone, my wallet, my clothes, bits and pieces out of my car, and whatever else they had of mine. The nasty one was there and I said, 'Where's my wallet?'

'What wallet?'

'The one you took out of my car.'

'We haven't got it.'

'Yes you have.'

'No, Annette, you probably lost that when you were out in the bush trying to bury Bevan.'

'You've got it all wrong.'

He said, 'Who says you can leave, anyway, what makes you think you're going anywhere?'

I said, 'Cut the crap. Next time you want to say anything to me you have to go through my lawyer.'

They didn't like that. They weren't very happy about it. They gave me my wallet before I left the station and they looked at me as if I was nothing. I was a bit scared of them then. They said I had to stay at the house. I said I couldn't because when I went there with the person who had picked me up from the station, it had tape all around it, like it was a crime scene. There were coppers all around the place and I couldn't get into the house. Mum gave me some money and I stayed in a caravan park down the road in one of their cabins.

I rang my lawyer, who said I had to go to court the next day. I asked what for and he told me. I'm not exactly sure what that was, but BJ was there and there was someone from legal aid there representing me because my lawyer couldn't get up there that day. So, BJ, myself and coppers sat there in the front of the court. BJ was under arrest, in custody and he couldn't go anywhere. He was handcuffed. There were cameras and reporters everywhere. It was quite shocking and embarrassing.

My legal aid representative stuffed it up, although I can't remember now what was said or what questions were asked. It was a long time ago. But I do remember as we walked out he said, 'I'll see you tomorrow,' and I said, 'Just go away, you're an idiot.' He had no clue what was going on. I'd never seen him before and I'd only spoken to him for about ten minutes before I walked into the courthouse. I didn't know what was going on. All I knew was that BJ had killed Bevan and he was under arrest. I was just thinking: I want my mum.

About four days after Bevan's death the cops drove sixteen hundred kilometres up to West Angelas mine to interview Ross at work. He was questioned by two cops who arrived at eleven o'clock at night. He was pulled off his grader and they spoke to him for about four hours. They asked him if he knew that this had happened. He said no, and they asked where he was at that time; it was as if they were setting up a conspiracy. They asked how he felt about Bevan and he replied, 'I'm glad he's dead, he used to bash my sister all the time and I don't care.' They must have left Hedland around seven o'clock at night and left West Angelas about three in the morning. One of the cops said to him, 'We didn't like the bloke anyway, mate. He deserved it.'

The police tried to create a theory that K's father, Ross and I had planned all this.

My parents ended up flying to Port Hedland from Bridgetown five or six days after it happened. By then I was in the hospital because I'd had a nervous breakdown.

CHAPTER FOURTEEN

Breakdown

At that point I was still thinking that BJ admitted doing it so what did I have to do with any of it? I just had a yearning to be with K. I wanted to be with K at his father's place, but I was told at the court that I had to sign in at the police station every day and I couldn't leave Port Hedland, and anyway, I had no car.

My next concern was how I was going to get from Port Hedland to South Hedland every day without a vehicle, but they gave me the white ute back, the one that BJ had put Bevan's body in. It was Bevan's ute, so they gave me the murder vehicle to use. They gave it back to me a couple of days later and it had blood and stuff all over it. One of my mates, Mick, came around and said he'd clean it for me. I had to drive twenty kilometres every day to sign in. They kept my car for a couple of weeks for forensics. But they followed me around all the time.

Eventually the police released the house where Bevan was killed. I was still reporting to them daily, and I had to stay in that house where he died. That wasn't good for my mental health. It was a bad situation and I had to clean up the house. Some friends came over and helped me; they found it upsetting and wouldn't let me do it on my own. It affected me. I couldn't sleep. It's difficult to explain but I had a hurricane of thoughts roaring through my head all the time but at the same time I couldn't keep a thought in my head. My brain felt like a scrambled egg. I couldn't think properly, I couldn't have a conversation, I couldn't keep up with what was being said, I couldn't understand it, I couldn't focus on what was anything.

My friends could see it, the state I was in, but I wasn't aware. Emotionally I felt like I was having slips and falls. I was suffering from anxiety and I couldn't eat, and when I tried, I'd just dry-retch. I was trying to keep it together. I went down to forty-five kilograms. One day I was going to the chemist and I ran into a friend, Mandy, whose kids were also into motocross. She said, 'I hear K's bike's up for sale.' I said yes, and I don't recall how the conversation went but eventually she said, 'You're not making any sense.' I said, 'Oh, yeah, well, if you want to look at the bike, I've got to go.' And I just cut it off.

I went into the chemist and he asked me, 'How are you going, Annette?' I said yes and something else, I've forgotten what, and he looked concerned and asked me if

I was OK. I said yes, and he said, 'You're not making any sense, go up to the hospital. Go and talk to someone there.' I wasn't on any medication and I'd started drinking, not a lot, but more than I was used to. I'd have drinks with my friends and then the next day I'd have more drinks with my friends. I started thinking, what's going on here? This isn't me. What's happening here? I had some pretty rough nights. I'd go out to a friend's place and as soon as I got there I'd be thinking, I don't want to be here. I'd go home and I'd think, I don't want to be here in this house where Bevan died. I was like the walking dead. It was like I had this shell, this body, but inside there was just this raving lunatic.

Everyone, all my friends and even Larry, Bevan's brother, were all supportive. Matt was just a few houses down the road and he came up and asked if he could get something of Bevan's. I told him he could have whatever he wanted. I'd bought Bevan a watch, it had cost around eight hundred dollars, and he said he wanted that and Bevan's necklace. He was crying and he said, 'I knew this would happen, but I thought it would be you.' All my close friends said the same thing. As soon as they heard someone had died on the street and all the cop cars were there, they all assumed Bevan had killed me. Everybody had thought that. Everybody.

The drink didn't help other than numbing me for a while. I'd go three days without sleep. My brain, well, I don't know. It was like I was full of adrenaline, on overload, and I was getting headaches all the time from it. The pharmacist was the first person to suggest I get help. All my friends as well as others would tell me I just needed support from friends, I was grieving, I'd get over it, it was normal. I'd say no, I don't feel normal, when will I get over it? I just can't carry this shit feeling around, it feels so bad. They'd say oh we know what it's like. I started getting angry. I'd say, no, you don't know what it's like. They'd tell me to settle down, I'd say fuck you because you don't get it.

Eventually they gave me my HiLux back. I don't know why they kept it so long, there was nothing in it.

When the pharmacist told me to go to the hospital, I wasn't happy with the idea. I didn't want to but I went anyway. It probably wasn't even much of a thought, I just went. I walked to the front desk and told the woman there that I needed to see someone and that my partner had died. She must have known who I was and she told me to wait a minute and went off and came back with a doctor who took me into a room to talk. I became quite friendly with him over the period I was in the hospital. He asked me what was going on and he said, 'Oh, you're the one whose partner died.' I just started rambling, blurting out all this shit and he said, 'When was the last time you had some sleep?' I said three days ago, then I'd ramble some more, constantly switching the conversation. He told me I'd need some sleeping tablets and that I needed to stay in hospital and take something to calm me down. I asked what was wrong with me and he told me I was grieving. I said, 'What?' I didn't understand that. I was crying, and I told him, 'I think I'm going around the twist.' He asked me all these questions and said, 'There's nothing wrong with you, you're not losing your mind, it's normal.' I asked, 'How is this normal? This isn't normal.'

I can't deal with that feeling, that horrible, disgusting feeling. If I lost K, I wouldn't survive that. It's one of my greatest fears.

This doctor was good to talk to. I booked into the hospital and was given some sleeping tablets and valium. I didn't have to stay there but I was getting lots of sleep and a lot of visitors, but I didn't remember any of them coming. They told me later that I was just zoned right out. I do remember Mum and Dave coming. He brought me some earrings, and I vaguely remember people visiting but no details. I could leave during the day and often would as I still had to report to the police station, but I'd always go back. They put me in the children's ward because it was nice and quiet. I was only there for four or five days. It was peaceful.

Dave had told me that if I ever wanted to talk about anything, he was there. I did talk to him a bit about it but not all of it. That was when I was a bit zoned out. My mum, on the other hand, was worried and she'd cry, she didn't understand. 'What's wrong with you?' she used to say.

And years later when I got out of jail she said, 'I realise what was wrong with you now. You were grieving.' At the time, she didn't want to know about it because she hated Bevan, she didn't care about what had happened to him. She was pleased he was gone after the way he'd treated her daughter. I can understand that now. She cared about me and was worried about me, but she didn't care what had happened to him. I wasn't glad he was gone, especially not like that, but I did feel relief I didn't have to put up with that anymore. I felt for his family, particularly his mother. He had a son but he never saw him.

I also worried about BJ and his family, and what was going to happen to him. At the same time, I didn't think anything was going to happen to him. In my little world, there'd been a fight, he'd told them what had happened, I'd told them what had happened and that was going to be the end of it. It didn't register in the slightest what was going to happen after that, I could never imagine that. I just thought, if you tell the truth then that's that, it would all be good. I hadn't considered what was coming and when it did, that was like a big, bloody bomb.

CHAPTER FIFTEEN

BACK TO KARRATHA

I just thought that BJ got into a fight. When I look at it now and see things on the news, I realise it happens all the time. It turns your world to shit. It could happen to anyone.

In the end, I felt I had to leave the hospital, I couldn't stay there forever. I thought I'd be OK, but I wasn't. The doctor said I could come back and talk to him anytime I liked, so I'd sometimes call him and have a yarn on the phone or I'd go up there and talk to him. Mum and Dave were staying in Port Hedland for a while so I thought, well, they're there, so everything's going to be OK, but it wasn't the case.

I started getting angry and having lots of arguments when people started to annoy me. I'd snap at my friends just during a normal conversation and at my mum when she told me I was drinking too much. I'd shout, 'Just leave me alone, mate, go away!' It got to the point where I didn't want to be around them. I didn't want to be around my family, I didn't want to be around my friends, I just wanted to disappear into a hole somewhere. I started to not care about myself, I was just devastated. And I wanted to see my son but I didn't want K to see me like that.

I'd ring him up all the time and say, 'How's it going, buddy, and what have you been doing?' and he'd tell me what he'd been up to and I'd just act normal and then I'd hang up the phone and feel so angry. I desperately wanted to see him.

About a month or more after that night, I phoned up my lawyer who I'd never met and told him I wanted to get out of Port Hedland, and most of all I wanted to get out of that house. I couldn't stay in that house. I thought I could hear Bevan talking to me there. I had some friends move in with me, they wanted to help me but I hated being there, it just did my head in. Living in the house where your partner has been killed is just sick. It was the last place I wanted to be. I told my lawyer I wanted to move to Karratha. K had been born there and I had a lot of friends there. It's about two hundred kilometres west of Port Hedland.

My lawyer tried to arrange it. I had to go to the South Hedland court, because the police were saying, no, we're not having this, you're not going anywhere. At the court the legal aid bloke was there. I told him to just go away, but he said I needed someone to represent me. I said, 'No I don't, you're just an idiot.' He was the same one I was given the first time I had to go to court. So I went to court, the coppers were there, the judge asked me what the suit was about. I told him that I was applying to move to Karratha. When he asked why, I told him I didn't want my son coming back here, I didn't want him to hear about what had happened, I didn't want him to know about it, it was all about protecting K. Also, I couldn't live in that house where my partner had died. I just can't do it. So he said, 'Alright, you can go, you can move there.' The police didn't like that.

In Karratha I still had to report daily to the police station but the police there were different. They weren't like the Port Hedland police, they were nowhere near as bad. Some of those Hedland coppers jumped up to detectives after that case; they were bullies.

While still in Port Hedland, I did go and see BJ in the Roebourne prison where he was being held, maybe a couple of weeks after that terrible night. There was nothing in my conditions that said I couldn't visit him. When I got there, they phoned the Port Hedland police, then they told me, 'You can't see him.' So, I just turned around and went back to Port Hedland.

I was only in Karratha for three or four months. K was back with me, he was in school, and K's father saw him all the time because he was living down the road in Pannawonica and coming over on his days off and I had all my friends there from the motocross trials and the

Karratha motocross club. I was still pretty fucked up but was trying to keep it together. I felt huge relief at getting away from Port Hedland, from getting away from those coppers, from getting away from that house. I didn't have to see Bevan's brother. The whole place just reminded me of it and I just didn't want to be there. It gave me a bit of distance from all of that.

I had my son back and his father visiting all the time. We'd go camping and fishing, we had fun. I was trying to be strong for K, and he sees me now as this strong person and nothing can hurt me. He sees me, as he says, as one of his life's pinnacles. I had a relationship breakup a little while ago and K was worried about me. I told him I'd be OK and he said, 'I know you will, you'll survive anything, you're strong.'

K's father rented me a house in Karratha and he paid the rent. It was a big four-bedroom house. A mate from Pannawonica moved in and rented a room. The house sat up on a bit of a hill and in front of it there was a big open area with the highway and dirt and spinifex, and there was a phone box down there. I started noticing that there were people down there all the time. It appeared to be workers fixing the phone box a lot. My phone sounded funny and my mum's phone sounded funny. I noticed that friends' phones sounded weird. I was talking to a friend in Bunbury and she said there was someone at the door. When she opened the door there were two detectives standing there.

They asked her who she was speaking to on the phone and she told them: Annette. They said, 'We know, we were listening to your phone conversation.' They were recording every single call I made on my mobile. Twenty-seven hours of recorded phone calls since the day I'd left the police station in Port Hedland. They tried to get them into court but there was nothing on them. That paperwork got thrown out of court when the judge refused to listen to twenty-seven hours of phone conversations. They were transcribed and he'd looked at the transcriptions and said there was nothing in them.

I was sitting in the Karratha shopping centre with K one day. I'd bought him a hot dog from Wendy's and we were sitting on a little bench and I saw these blokes walking through the centre. They were quite big men. They looked like rugby players but they were in suits. They came over to me and asked me how I was going.

I said, 'Ah, you're from Port Hedland.'

One of them squatted down in front of me and said, 'How's everything going?'

'Alright.'

'And who's this young man,' looking at K.

'You know who it is.'

'How're you going, K? You're a pretty good motocross rider, aren't you?'

I was furious. K said, 'Yeah.'

'Isn't he, Annette?'

'Yeah.'

'You came first yesterday at the motocross.'

I looked at him.

'Yeah, we were at the motocross, Annette.'

I'd see them in the rear vision mirror of my car as they followed me around. They were letting me know that they were there. But instead of just following me and listening to my phone calls, they were now approaching me. It was intimidating. Sometimes K's father would call me and ask me to phone him back from a phone box. They brought that up and tried to make a big deal of it, asking why I had done that. I told them it was none of their business what I said on the phone. They went to Mum and Dave's and questioned my mum, saying they wanted to know what a certain conversation was about. She told them it had nothing to do with them and refused to say anything. They didn't like that.

About a week after Bevan died, two plain clothes detectives pulled me over at the Port Hedland shopping centre. I hopped out and they said they wanted to look at my car and I said, 'Here we go again.' They said, 'You've got to sign in at the South Hedland police station today, don't you?' and I said, 'Yeah, every day and you know it,' and they said, 'Well you won't be driving this much longer,' and when I asked why not, they looked it over and said there was that little rip in the bench seat. I said, 'I'll just put a seat cover over it.' They said, no, they'd put a yellow sticker on it for having a little tiny rip on the front seat, so then I didn't have a car, did I. A yellow sticker is something the police issue which gives you a week, maybe two, to fix up whatever is wrong. It must go over the pits for a complete examination, so if they find anything else wrong, they won't pass it, leaving you without a car.

I rang the bloke at the pits, and I got my mate Mick to take it out there. The bloke from the pits called me back and told me to just throw a seat cover on it. I agreed. Then he called back to say the police had been there and had told him not to pass my vehicle over the pits or they would take his business licence off him. Great, I thought, this is just getting worse and worse!

The police had told me they didn't know who had killed Bevan, it could have been BJ or it could have been me. BJ had told them he did it when they pulled him up on the side of the road. He told them everything, he didn't hold back on anything. They'd taken him back to the house and he'd walked them through everything that had happened, the what and the where. But no, they wanted to blame it on me. They'd collected all the forensics from me but they had been sent down to Perth for analysis. The way I was seeing it, they knew he'd done it. He was covered in Bevan's blood for one, there was nothing at all on me.

When the police wouldn't let my car out of the pits, my parents paid for me to get a hire car, so I was still able to go to the police station for the daily sign in, but often they'd tell me I had to wait for the so-and-so or the this-or-that. It was just a headache. I took my Mum and Dave with me to sign in and they were just horrible to her, and to Dave, just terrible. I said to Mum, 'See?' and Dave just said, 'What the hell's going on here?'

CHAPTER SIXTEEN

Arrest

There was a big motocross event in Karratha. There were hundreds of people there to see events like big dirt drag and other such things. K and some other kids, myself and friends who were involved in the motocross club were there putting up banners and cleaning up the motocross track, getting everything ready for the event. It was going to start the next day and K's father was there too. We weren't together, he was there for K, but we got on well and he was quite protective of me after all this had happened.

I was standing near some tables and someone came up behind me and tapped me on the shoulder. I turned around and a detective was standing there along with three other detectives from Karratha and Port Hedland. There was one big, fat one and he said, 'Do you remember me?' 'Of course I remember you.' 'I'm charging you for the wilful murder of [Bevan].'

I looked straight over to where K's father was, about twenty to fifty metres away, and he and the others all started walking towards me. I must have had this look on my face. I started walking backwards. I think I was hoping there was a big hole behind me and I'd just fall into it and disappear. The cop said, 'Where are you going, Annette?'

My mates arrived and asked what was going on and the cop said, 'Back it up a bit, she's been charged with wilful murder,' and I said, 'No I'm not, that's ridiculous!' They said I had to come down to the Karratha police station. I had the sickest feeling in my stomach. K started running over to see what was happening. He would have been about seven. He asked me what was going on and I told him to wait a minute. I turned to the cops and told them I wasn't going anywhere with them. 'I haven't done what you've said I've done.'

That's when I knew I was getting the blame for it. That hit me hard, I almost collapsed. They told me to get in the police car but I said I'd drive my own. They agreed but told me they'd follow me. I said I wanted to say goodbye to my son and they said, 'No you're not, don't you touch him.' K was running towards me screaming and I couldn't even say goodbye. Not for one minute did I ever think this would happen, my whole world caved in. K was screaming and I was crying, it was bad. It broke my heart.

All the other people were standing there. These were my friends, people I was quite close to. They all knew what had happened, they all knew Bevan before he died, they'd known K's father for a long time and they'd known K since he was born. Some of them demanded to know what was going on and they were told, 'You stand over there, and you, stand over there.' It was humiliating but I didn't care about the humiliation, it was the look on K's face. He knew Bevan had died; I had told him that BJ had accidentally killed him in a fight. That was all he knew. These people were quite protective of K and it was good, they sort of formed a circle of protection around him.

I thought I was going to go back to the police station and they'd run through all the same stupid interviews again and I thought I wouldn't be staying there because why would I be staying there? It wasn't real. I was thinking, did they really say that shit? What's going on here? And everything went pear-shaped after that. Big time.

On the drive to the station my mind was only on K. What would I do? He lived with me and his dad lived two hundred kilometres away in Pannawonica. I was surprised they let me drive myself but I figured that they were going to go through my car and I said that when we got there, but they said, no, they needed a warrant to do that. When K's father arrived, he said they'd been through my car.

When we arrived at the station I parked and they parked behind me and they took me to a room and that big, fat copper was there. I hated him, he was such an arsehole. He and two other detectives were in there and they said that this was the last chance to talk to them and that they didn't believe me.

The fat one leaned over and hissed in my ear, 'Do you know that when you get out of jail your son will be thirty-seven years old. You are going to get life for this, you may as well kiss him goodbye.' And then, 'In actual fact you won't get to kiss him goodbye because you're not going to see him again.'

That's when I got angry and I said, 'So I can't even say goodbye to my son?'

'Nuh! This is your last chance to talk to us,' so I told them again what had happened and they said again, 'We're charging you for wilful murder and we're going to send you up to Roebourne.'

That's a prison about forty kilometres out of Port Karratha.

'From there you're going to go to Bandyup.'

'What's that?'

'You know what that is.'

'No, I don't.'

'It's a women's prison in Perth.'

'I'm not going there.'

'Your son will be thirty-seven years old when you get out of prison, he'll be an adult. If you don't start telling us what's been going on...'

'I've told you. I've been repeating myself and repeating myself and repeating myself again.'

'We've seen BJ and we got a statement off him.' They wanted me to sign it.

I had a look through it and told them I wasn't signing it because that's not what happened. I said, 'I don't believe that's come out of BJ's mouth.' It said things like he'd gone there to kill Bevan, and I'd asked BJ to kill him, and that we'd planned to go and bury his body, just crap. 'Sign it now and we might not send you to Bandyup.' 'I'm not signing it. I don't believe BJ signed this because it's just not true.' 'Sign it!' I didn't.

Once again, I wasn't under arrest, I was being charged. This meant they hadn't read me my rights.

At the station, I ran into a copper who said, 'Hello, Annette. You don't know who I am, do you?' I said no, and he told me his name. He used to be my brother's best friend when they were kids and he used to come around our house all the time, and here he was, a copper. I thought great! How embarrassing! I hadn't seen him since I was about seven.

I also had a mate, Richard, from when we were in Karratha. He was from England but he'd been in Australia for a long time. He used to work at the motorbike shop that sponsored K for motocross. They questioned him because he was the one who took K at the track when the police came for me. He was like K's godfather and K's father was going to pick him up from Richard's place after he'd finished at the police station with me, and take him back to Pannawonica. They questioned Richard and they sent him back to England with a hundred dollars in his pocket because he wouldn't sign a statement. They questioned him and said he must have known what went on, because we were good friends.

They said to him, 'We know you've been talking to Annette.'

'Annette and I talk but she hasn't told me anything like what's written on that piece of paper.'

'OK, then we're going to send you down to the detention centre in Perth because you're an illegal immigrant from a long time ago.'

'I've been here for twenty years.'

He had a job, a house, a girlfriend in Karratha. They sent him down to the immigration centre in Perth when I was in prison and they sat him down and said, 'If you don't sign this statement saying that this is what Annette told you, we're sending you back to England.' And they sent him back to England where he still lives to this day, never to come back. I've still got letters written by him from England.

That was another big kick to my heart because he was a good friend. And heartbreaking for K too. He had looked after K for a couple of weeks when I was in jail. He was K's godfather and he used to live behind me. He rang me a few times when I was in prison. He was crying and very upset. I said, 'I'm sorry.' He said, 'It's not your fault, I don't blame you.' We've lost touch now but I used to get letters from him.

I was probably at the station for an hour or two. They charged me, then put me in a van and took me to Roebourne jail, thirty-one kilometres east of Karratha. I sat in the van looking out the back window and watched Karratha disappear into a tiny little speck as the tears rolled down my face. My mind was on K.

The gates opened and the van drove through. I was handed over to a male and female officer who didn't say a word. I was told I had to go through to a room and take my clothes off and have a shower. I thought, how fucking degrading. By now I was no longer crying, I was angry. Two female prison officers stood by, one telling me what to do and giving me nit shampoo to put through my hair. I told them, 'I'm not taking my clothes off in front of you!' They said I had to. One of them looked like a bloke. They stared at me as I took my clothes off. I said, 'Having a good look, are you?' What kind of person does this fucking job?

I was then told I had to squat over a mirror. I refused. 'I'm not doing that! You do it! If you want me to do that, you're going to have to make me do it because I'm not doing it. I'm not even fucking supposed to be here, I'm not doing it. You squat over the mirror because I'm not, I'm not doing it!'

I was so angry. They laughed and said, 'Isn't this one little miss attitude.' I didn't have to squat over the mirror.

They took me into another room and I was to pick some clothes out, but because I'm so little, nothing fitted me. The clothes were too big on me, but what do you do? They were tracksuits and that's in fifty degree heat up there. I followed the officers out into an area where everyone was playing basketball, men and women together. Every one of them was Aboriginal. I was hoping I'd see BJ because I knew he was there somewhere. Everyone stopped and stared. I spotted about five females in this huge number of people. I was escorted across to a big complex with a huge gate. This was the women's section; the male's section must have been over the other side of the prison so you don't get locked up with men. Inside there was a big concrete area that had five cells either side and they faced each other. About five metres away were another five cells facing each other. This was the maximum-security area and I realised there was no-one in there because they were out exercising. What I didn't realise was that this was where I was going to be staying. I wasn't going out that gate because this was maximum security. It was like being in a zoo, all concrete. They'd come and hose the floors down. The rooms had no air conditioning and it was intensely hot.

Those not in maximum security, those who weren't in for murder, could go out and intermingle but at nights they had to come back and were locked in the area I was in. But I wasn't allowed out that gate. No-one spoke to me at first, they just stared. At dinnertime, they brought the food in alfoil trays. It was then that Judy, the girl opposite me, came over. Her skin was so black that sometimes all you could see was the whites of her eyes.

She asked, ''Ow ya goin', mate.'

'Yeah, fucking great.'

'What are you doin' in 'ere?'

'Apparently wilful murder.'

'Aw, you're the one that was on the TV.'

I said yep and then it was small talk. She asked if I had any family, did I have any kids, and that was when I started crying. She tried to console me, saying I'd be alright. She said she was looking at me when I came in and thought, 'I don't want to go near her!' just from the look on my face. I had been angry. Judy was in for being drunk and disorderly. She turned out to be funny.

She ended up in Bandyup. I was walking back from the gardens where I used to work and she yelled out, 'Hey, old mate!' I said, 'What are you doing here?' and then I said, 'Thank God you're here!' I was so happy to see her. She came and worked in the gardens with me but all the other Aboriginal women hated her for hanging around with white people. Most of them were of mixed blood and are lighter skinned and they fear the blacks from up north. I think maybe because they're ashamed. The ones up north might sniff a bit of petrol but they're not on crack and breaking into people's houses and cars. At Roebourne there were a couple of other women apart from Judy who'd come over for a yarn and bum some cigarettes. Otherwise I was pretty much left alone.

The food was disgusting. I didn't eat it that first night, I gave it to Judy when she said, 'If you don't want it, I'll have it!' I lost a lot of weight. I went down to forty-five kilos.

I was the only one in for murder so I was alone much of the day as the others all went out into the communal area outside. They lock the doors at seven o'clock. If you use the toilet, you're in full view of anyone passing by. Most of the guards are men. I didn't have a lot to do with them because I wasn't allowed out of my cell, but they weren't too bad. You can't have anything to read. They have a library and a deli but I couldn't go there either because I was in maximum security. I just sat there day after day after day in that unbearable heat. K, Bevan, my family, what happened, what was going to happen, how fucked up my life was, the thoughts tumbled around and around in my head. I wanted to see K's father.

I did have some visitors. K came to see me with a mate. A couple of friends from Karratha came. K's father came to see me but I didn't get to see him. I knew that he'd come but another mate had come to see me when he'd pulled up, and the detectives were there seeing BJ. It was weird because I was standing near this fence and I could see BJ. I was standing in those cells and there was a big fence there and another behind it. I could see him walking over there across this lawn. I yelled out to him. He came over to the farthest fence and said g'day.

I said, 'What are you doing out there? How come you're out there and I'm in here?'

He said, 'What do you mean?'

'How come you're allowed to wander around?'

'I'm on my way to the library.'

'Did you get any visitors today?'

'Yeah, K's father was supposed to come and see me.'

'Oh right. But the detectives came and saw you, didn't they?'

'Yeah.'

'Right, well how come you're out there and I'm in here?'

'I don't know.'

'I do recall that you're the one who did this so how come I'm getting punished for it? You'd better fix this up because I want out of here and I want to see my son, BJ.'

Something in the pit of my stomach suddenly didn't trust him, this long-term friend of mine. I didn't trust him and I thought, 'You're not pinning this shit on me.' As it turned out that was not what was going on at all.

But I was dirty about that. Why are you a free-range chicken in this big bloody chicken pen and I'm locked in this hole? So, I rang my lawyer up. I asked him what was going on. He didn't know, he was surprised, but it turned out they'd charged BJ with grievous bodily harm and me with wilful murder. That was the first I'd heard about that.

This was after about four days in Roebourne. The next day BJ was put in maximum security as well. I still don't understand that. They pull BJ up on the road with Bevan and I'm in jail on murder and he's got grievous bodily harm.

I found out that they'd upgraded him to wilful murder from BJ himself when I saw him in court. I was in Roebourne for about two weeks. Two weeks with nothing to read, nothing to do, they'd have barbecues that I couldn't go to because I was in maximum security. I was just stuck in that concrete. My parents didn't come because they were down in Bridgetown. Now I look back on it and wonder how I ever did it because that nearly drove me insane.

CHAPTER SEVENTEEN

Inside

This is the phone system in Roebourne: they give you a piece of paper and you can write up to four, maybe five phone numbers that you can put in their phone. They then give you a code. The phone is like a big silver box and it's got numbers from zero to nine and you put your code in and you put each of your phone numbers under a number, say K's number into number one, Mum's underneath number two, and so on, you just press that number and it will call the number that's in there. They record all your calls but you can only talk for ten minutes and then the phone cuts out.

You can make as many calls as you've got money for in there. If someone comes and visits you and they give you money, you can give it to the officers or administration and they'll put it on your phone account. If you don't get visitors or if nobody brings you money, then it's bad luck, no phone calls. It's the same in Bandyup, if you don't get given money or if you don't work in there, you can't put any money on your phone and you can't go down to the canteen and get smokes or anything. So, you have to work in there. You work or you get nothing.

When I was in Crisis Care in Bandyup at the beginning, I wasn't in their phone system and I'd just ask for a phone call and they'd give me one or two, then I'd ask for another one and they'd just say no. Eventually they used K against me. If they decided I had an attitude, which I did when they pissed me off, they'd say, 'When your son comes down, Annette, do you want to see him or do you not want to see him? Do you want to make a phone call to him or do you not want to make a phone call to him?' It was terrible emotional blackmail all the time.

When I was first in Crisis Care, I met an officer called Mr Lawler. He was quite a big bloke and he was the prosecutor in there, so he was a prison officer but also a prosecutor. You can go to court in prison, how ridiculous. So, if you get into trouble in prison, if you get caught with drugs or anything, he's the one who comes and sees you. He was one of the first officers I saw in Bandyup and he was always nice to me. I just felt a connection with him as he seemed to know how I was feeling. And I knew that he was OK. He was the one who organised a special visit for my mum and my sister to come into the Crisis Care place to see me. He was nice to them and I hadn't seen my mum for ages and I hadn't seen Dianne for a couple of years.

I was in Crisis Care for about a week. They've only got six cells there and they've got padded cells for people who lose it. Just around the corner in that same unit is Isolation. Where you go when you're naughty. The padded cells get used a lot because there are people in there from Graylands Psychiatric Hospital because it's full, so the overflow end up in prison. You don't realise when you're in Crisis Care where you are, it's not until you step outside when your time's up and you see the rest of the place and you just think, oh no!

So after your week is up you're turfed out and put in with the general prison population. It's a women's only prison. The Norma Streams and all the raving lunatics are in there. There are two big gates and in between those gates there's an office. There are thirty rooms on one side of the office with big walls around them, and thirty rooms on the other side of the office, and then there's a big two-storey building across from that one that's full of people, and then you've got self-care, the accommodation for the Norma Streams and all the killers that get special treatment from everybody. They're still in the general population but at night they go up there in their special little village where they've got their pool table and coke machines and they can do their own cooking and have their own food that they want. They get treated better than everybody else. These are the killers, the paedophiles, the lifers who have killed young children.

I was in custody on remand, which means I was being held in prison until my trial. I was innocent until proven guilty according to our laws, and here I was holed up with these psychopaths and murderers. And the people who had kidnapped, murdered, cut people's eyeballs out, tortured – they get the better treatment. I could not understand it. I thought, hang on, I'm on remand and the trash of society, the most despicable human beings, have got a nice little village up there that I'm not allowed to enter. They can come down and be where we are, but it's a one-way street. It's insane. They get the best jobs in the prison, they can own and wear their own clothes, they're allowed to keep presents. If K came and visited me and wanted to give me a present, I wasn't allowed to have it, it goes to administration for when you leave, but they're allowed to keep stuff. If you asked what was going on here, why was this happening, you'd be in trouble, you were a troublemaker. The lifers may as well have run the prison; the warden would go to them to ask their opinions, 'What do you think we should do here? How do you think we should do this?'

Who are these people? These are people like Tammie Sherratt who, with her boyfriend, knocked a fourteen-year-old boy off his trail bike and tortured and killed him. They tied him to a tree, they cracked his skull with a rock, they stabbed his chest with a samurai sword, a rope was tied around his neck, he was strangled and his heart was torn when one of them trod on his back. Norma Stream who, with her partner, raped and murdered four young women in a month. There would have been more if the fifth one, a teenager, hadn't escaped. Janine Lipster and her mate, who used to be prostitutes at a brothel, killed a fifteen-year-old boy and put him in the boot of the car and buried him. These are just freaks, pure evil. This is what they call punishing somebody, is it?

Norma Stream's old, she doesn't have to worry about paying rent, she's doing fine in there, everybody's a bit scared of her or something, I don't know, she's the head librarian. I told her to fuck off when I was in there. 'Get away from me. Get the fuck away. Get away, mate.' Some of them served at the canteen. The worst prisoners got the best jobs. You only have to work a couple of hours at meal times if you work in the canteen. I was working in the gardens; it's like being in the army. I've never had such muscles in my life. Working out in the rain and in the stinking heat, whipper snipping and digging and mowing lawns. I didn't mind it because it was good exercise and it was outside, but I thought, if you murdered my son, I'd want to see you in a hole in isolation buried up to your neck.

I used to go up there to do the gardening. They had barbecues up there. I met Marnie Chandler. In the papers, it said she was the first female hit woman. She killed someone because she got paid five hundred dollars. She was in there for life. She was eighteen when she went in, she's been there about thirty years. She'd never seen an ATM, never seen a credit card, computer, or mobile phone. I became quite friendly with her for some reason. I'd gone up to do some whipper snipping and was sitting on a bench putting some more line in the whipper snipper when she came and sat next to me.

After the hellos, she said, 'I've seen you around. What are you in here for.'

I'd never told anyone what I was in there for, I just used to say 'stuff'. So I told her, 'Stuff.'

'Oh yeah, I saw it in the paper. You don't talk to many people, do you.'

'Nah, it doesn't really interest me.'

And then she offered me a smoke. After that I'd quite often see her. It was weird because I sort of became mates with her. I suppose I could talk to her about stuff. She was a mate. She used to say, 'What are you doing here? You're more intelligent than the average person here.' 'Yeah,' I'd say, 'that's because it's a sea of idiots here, a big blue sea of idiots.'

She got to know about K. She said if I ever wanted to talk, she was there. When I asked her what she was in for she said she'd tell me one day. And she did. Some bloke got her to kill this girl and make it seem like it was an accident and everyone thought it was a suicide. Then he went and blabbed to everybody and actually blamed it on her and she was going to go to jail forever and he was going to get off scot-free. So, her lawyer told her that when she went to court she was to plead not guilty, and she asked what would happen to her. He said, 'Well he'll walk but you might get a couple of years.' When she went to court, she pleaded guilty and it took him with her. She said she has a lot of remorse for the killing. She was eighteen when she did it. She lost her family because of it, although her son comes and visits her.

It was strange, later when I was in the hospital with my sister, Marnie walked in. I said, 'You got out of there?' She said, 'Yep.' She was happy and laughing. She said, 'You know what? I was so lucky I met you because when you got breast cancer I went and got checked and I had bad breast cancer. I've just had my boobs cut off. Thanks to you, I didn't die. You must have been in there for a reason.' She was happy. She'd come up for parole and she lives out in the country in a little house now.

I had a lot of acquaintances in there but I only had a small number of tight-knit friends. One was Lisa. Lisa was a mate and I still talk to her now. She was in there for three years or so. Her partner got shot, it was a domestic violence situation. Joan, she was in there for drugs, which was unusual, I don't usually hang around with people like that, but I liked her. She had a little baby when she got out. I still have contact with her. Shirley was another and she got engaged to my brother. She was in for drunk driving. There was Alice, a good mate I still talk to, she was in for armed robbery. A knife at a service station. There was Emma who was in for drunk driving after losing her licence about five times. She's down in Melbourne now. I was quite friendly with her. All these women had first time convictions, they all worked in the gardens with me and they're all out and living normal lives now. I had some pretty low times in there so I was lucky they were around, they helped me a lot. When I got out, they were still in there and I got lots of mail from them.

When I first arrived, I felt a bit strange about it, but my friends in there and even the female psychologist said, 'There's something about you.' She said, 'It's like looking out at a paddock and the sheep are all over there on that side of the fence, but they all want to be around you. It's like you've got this shining thing. Someone's looking after you.' Because I was probably one of the only people in there who didn't have a big problem with the other inmates. I got into two fights but apart from that nothing. One of the two fights happened when I was ringing K. I was in the phone box talking to him and this Aboriginal woman came up and told me to get off the phone. This was maybe the third day I was there. I told her no, that I was talking. She repeated, 'Get off the phone.' K asked me who that was. I said, 'Just a minute.' I told her I was talking to my son. She said, 'Well give me the phone.' I said no and she just started smashing me in the head. I said to K, 'I've got to go.' She kept on punching me in the head. I said, 'Fuck this!' and she said, 'You have to learn to know that what is yours is mine!'

You start off in A block when you first get in there and if you behave yourself they'll put you in B block and if you continue to behave yourself you get moved into B and C, the better wings of the building. If you get into a fight or someone punches you in the head or anything, you get kicked out and both of you go to isolation.

I started yelling obscenities at this woman, then went to my room and she came to the door and screamed at me that she was going to kick me in the... I can't write it, it's too disgusting. Some of them say the filthiest stuff, I'd never heard things like that. I said, 'If you come in here, I'm kicking you straight back out! Don't you *ever* do that again! *Ever!* Where I come from you sit on the oval picking nits out of each other's hair. Don't you fucking do that again! I'm not scared of you!' She just looked at me, then she walked off. She never did that again. I knew that I couldn't let them get away with that, it doesn't matter what the consequences are, because they used to gang up on people, like packs of dogs. I used to think, well what are they going to do? Beat me up? Well, Bevan used to do that all the time so I suppose that's not going to hurt. And I didn't care, I just wanted to be left alone.

The second time was when I was in that C and D wing where you have your own shower in your room, whereas in the other blocks you have to share showers. I'd just had a shower after coming in all dirty and sweaty from the gardens, and I was about to have a visit from K. I'd spilt a bit of butter and I went to put my coffee cup in the sink. They always have this person that serves the food up. I turned around from the sink and she headbutted me in the nose and split it open. She was screaming in my face too. 'You fuckin' white cunt, clean the fuckin' place up, who spilt the fuckin' butter? You did, didn't ya?' I'm standing there with this cracked nose and the officers just stand and watch it. I said, 'Thanks very fucking much for that! I've got a meeting with my son in about five seconds. I'll give you that one,' and I yelled, 'but it's not fucking happening again! Not. Happening. Again!' I was yelling full on and I don't do that very often. I thought, 'Don't scream in my face, I'll scream at you too.' Then I turned up for the visit and K asked me what happened. I got a big split nose and a black eye after that. I thought, great. She came and apologised when I went back.

She said, 'Sorry.'

'Sorry? That doesn't really cut it, does it?'

'I'm coming up for parole in the next couple of days.'

'Really? That's your bad luck isn't it. I don't care, mate.' I started yelling, 'I'm sick of this! Sick of this fucking joint!'

I started throwing stuff around then and they came and put me in isolation. So, I get cracked on the nose and screamed at, I scream back and I get put in isolation because I'm a threat to everybody. But they were the only two times. I got into a few small arguments but nothing too hectic. I don't know what it was and the officers used to comment on it saying, 'You know, you can be sitting there and there'll be fights going on around and it's like you've got this little ring around you that people are too scared to come into.' I don't know what it was, I didn't get into much trouble there. Well, I got into trouble, I certainly wasn't an angel in there, but it was mainly about wanting to see K or them not letting me have my visits.

I had a few run-ins with K's dad about K spending time by himself. They only came up to visit me together once and that was when I had cancer. I said to him, 'I've got custody of him, even though I'm inside on remand, I've still got custody and if you can't look after him and do the right thing I'm going to give him to Mum.' He didn't like that. I don't know if I did the right thing now or not. But he had all these friends in Pannawonica, it's a closed town, people don't live there unless they work for the mine. All his friends were there, they all knew about what had happened, so they sort of took care of him, I think, in some ways. I didn't want to take him away from his dad either. They needed each other at that time. His dad's quite strict with him too so I don't know. I'd ring him up sometimes and he'd be crying and K's father was at work and he'd been bitten on the eye by a hornet and he'd been riding around on his pushbike and his dad's at work. Those sorts of things were horrible to listen to, because you couldn't ring after seven o'clock at night. But I wrote K a letter every single day. And he wrote me lots of letters. It might just be a few lines saying, 'Hi Mum, I got bitten by a bee today and anyway I've got to go because I'm going camping.' Just a couple of lines.

When I moved house down to here, I was going through K's cupboards and he had a shoe box in there with every single letter that I wrote. And he's still got them. Sometimes I'd make him cards or write little poems. I'd always say to him, 'Smile, K, life's good.' I never told him it was bad in there; he just knew I worked in the gardens. Even if I was all broken and twisted inside, I'd always say I'm alright. I'm alright. 'Are you alright, Mum?' 'Yeah, I'm alright.' 'Are you sure?' 'Yeah, I'm alright.'

He knows a few things about what I'd done in there, like the time I had my TV taken off me and I threw it over the balcony and smashed it because they were horrible to me. They used to punish me all the time for nothing and I'd end up in isolation for no reason, stuff like that. They'd use K against me all the time and they didn't like you having mates in there – they'd break you up because they reckoned you were a gang. I was happy working with my friends in the gardens and the head of security broke us up, making one work in the kitchen, one here, one there. I'd complain, what? We're not doing anything, just going to work and hanging out. He said, 'No, you're conspiring.

I can see your mind ticking over all the time, Annette.' They used to say to me, 'Everyone in here cuts the steak with the grain, you cut it against the grain.' They said, 'We don't have people like you in here, because you're not the same as them.' They're all drugged up and they don't get people in there who haven't been in trouble before. They don't like it. They don't like someone with a little bit of intelligence or with a bit of spirit.

When the prison officers would look at me like I was a piece of rubbish or talk to me in a degrading or bullying way, I'd stand up to them. They'd say, 'I don't know who you think you're talking to.' So, I had no problem saying it to them. They'd say, 'Don't talk to me like that,' and I'd say, 'Well, you talk to me like that and I'll treat you like you treat me. Don't forget, outside of here I had a life. I had a life just like you. So, I don't appreciate it. If you want me to treat you decently, then treat me decently. Just because you're an officer in a prison and you lock people up doesn't make you better than anybody else.' They'd say, 'Is that right. Is that a fact. Then what are you doing in here? You'd better get used to being in here because this is where you're staying so who are you going to tell about how we treat you here? You're not getting out of here.' I said, 'You people are cracked, nobody knows what goes on in here, you treat people like animals.' Not all of them, but most of them.

There was no-one else in there that claimed to be innocent. The staff didn't believe that I was but my friends in there knew. I made some good friends in Bandyup that I still talk to now; they'd be the only people I'd talk to about it.

There was a bit of sexual activity between prisoners and male officers going on in there. That was a way to get special favours. Everyone knew who was having it off with who. Fred Smith was head of security, the one who would put me down the back all the time. He would always take this woman Janine Lipster with him. She was in there for life, she killed a fifteen-year-old boy, and I always thought there was something going on with them. The whole prison knew; they were always together. When I was at Dianne's place after the trial, I had the internal investigators come and see me. They were investigating him and they had been for three years. He got moved out of there, I think he was transferred to another jail, it was in the papers. I think he was a little bit scared of me. He always used to yell at me for nothing and punish me. He would poke me in the chest and he was physically aggressive.

The officers knew there were drugs in the prison. There was a lot there. They'd get passed over on visits or they'd get thrown in the gardens. People would know when there was going to be a drop and they'd know you worked in the gardens and get you to pick them up for them. Once you'd done it once, they'd expect you to do it all the time.

I'd say, nope, I'm not doing it. They'd say, 'But you work in the gardens.' I'd say, 'So what? I'm not doing that.' They'd throw it over in tennis balls and all kinds of stuff. I don't understand it. People would come in with a heroin addiction and they'd put them on a methadone program. I used to think, where's my six-pack? As far as I'm concerned, they're in there as a punishment, they shouldn't be giving them drugs, what sort of bullshit's that? If it's good enough for them to have that, where's my six-pack? They'd say, 'Don't be ridiculous, Annette.' I'd say, 'I'm not being ridiculous. I don't understand it, these people come in and they're heroin addicts and they're given methadone.'

One time some friends had some pot in there. They asked me to go down there and share a smoke. I said, no, I'm not doing that shit. After a while I thought, oh well, I'd just do it the once because I was so bored in there, there was nothing to do. Never again. I ended up so paranoid, I went straight to my room. I thought, what's happening here? It was bad. I hadn't touched it since before K was born, when we went to Amsterdam. My friends said, 'What's wrong with you?' I said, 'All kinds of stuff!' They just laughed at me and said I was one of the funniest people they'd ever met.

I had some good times in there, I suppose, you just had to make the most of it. One time a friend and I were whipper snipping down the back and my friend poured petrol on a big palm tree outside the laundry and she lit it up. There was a huge fire in the big palm tree. An Aboriginal girl was shouting, 'Those white girls did that, aye!' So they came up and asked me if I did that. 'Did what?' 'You lit that palm tree up, didn't you?' 'That's right, blame everything on me, I always get the blame.' 'But you did do it, didn't you?' 'Where would I get the fuel from?' 'Out of the whipper snipper.' I said to them, 'Fuck me, I'm in on a wilful murder charge, I'm walking around in here with axes, saws, screwdrivers, whipper snippers.'

Another time we were down there doing fences and some whipper snipping and there's a medical centre there with tinted windows so you can't see in. It was a hot day and I needed a drink of water badly. I said to my friend Lisa, 'I'm going to get over that fence and get some water.' She said, 'You can't do that. How are you going to get over?' I said, 'I'll dig a hole under the fence.' It was sandy there and I had a shovel with me. You can't get out of the place, you can just get into another part of the prison and there was a tap on the other side. So, I dug a hole and I squeezed into it like a snake. I got to the other side and I took my hat off and I washed my face down and drank heaps of water, then I went back under the fence and I heard, 'Ms Murcott, can you come to the office!' I thought, righto, what's this all about, not even thinking it was about that, and they said, 'We were standing over at the medical centre and we could see you. You dug a hole like a rabbit and got under the fence, and then you went back under there again,' and I said, 'I was thirsty.' They said, 'You can't do that, you've got to go down to isolation.' I thought, good grief, all I wanted was some water. They said, 'You're the only person who does shit like that. You've got to do it, don't you?' And then they put it down as an attempted escape.

At the Visitor Centre, you can have contact visits with people and then you can have non-contact visits with people if you're naughty, if the drug dog sits on somebody or something like that, and to get out of there they've got to unlock the door and let you out. But they'll leave you in there and it's so stinking hot. But there are windows in there that you can open, and I was there with this woman, Marnie Chandler, she was the hit woman who was in for thirty years, so she was about sixty years old. I said, 'God it's hot in here. I'm getting out that window.' She said, 'You can't do that! Don't get out there!' So I climbed out and she climbed out. Then some officers came along and said, 'What do you think you two are doing?' I said, 'Leaving the Visitor Centre.' They said, 'You can't do that shit aye.' I said, 'Well, it was bloody hot.' They said, 'We'll come back in and let you out.' I said, 'Yeah, like an hour later. It's stinking hot in there.' Marnie Chandler was living in the good part of the prison, and they kicked her out of her room and put her in a cell next to mine. She was like, 'Good on you, Annette,' and I said, 'Oh well.' And they put that down as an attempted escape.

They lock up the cells at ten to seven. They come along and check all your rooms at seven o'clock and one day I said to Lisa, 'I'm going to hide in the laundry just to see what they do.' She said, 'I'll hide in there too, I'll hide in there too!' They've got these big washing machines and dryers in there so we went into the laundry room and we could hear them doing all their lock-up and then we could hear all these officers running past the laundry. We were laughing, we couldn't stop. We could hear them on the radio saying Lisa and I had gone missing. I said, 'Just let them keep running around for a bit, so we did and they were running around and running around and running around. Then I yelled out, 'I'm in here!' And they unlocked the door and came in and started shouting, 'You fucking idiots, what do you think you're playing at?' I said, 'Ah, you're the ones who locked us in there, we've been trying to get out.' Fuck me dead. Hide in the laundry and give them something to do. See how long it takes them to find out you're missing, see if they care. Lisa and I were just laughing and laughing. They were looking for us for half an hour. It was like a code red then for people missing, they think you've escaped. They're the ones who locked us in the laundry. I got, 'You think you're funny, don't you, Murcott?' 'Well, it is pretty funny when you look at it.'

If you've got a can of cool drink, other inmates want it or they want to have a drink out of it, so they'll pick a fight with you. A lot of these people have hepatitis B or syphilis or other diseases – I'm not drinking out of the same can as them. I would buy up all the tokens for seventy or eighty dollars when they emptied the drink dispenser and would give them to friends if they wanted a can of coke, or if I wanted something that someone else had like rollie papers or something like that. We'd do a swap; it was a bartering system in there. It stops fights too, because they'd see you going to the coke machine and they'd come and stand behind you or stand next to you because they were going to smack you in the head for a can of coke, there was going to be a big thing about it, so I'd just give them a coke token and then every time they saw me after that they'd just say, 'How you going, Annette?' and they'd leave me alone. I'd give tokens to some people and sell them to others, depending on who they were. It would keep the peace. It's like when you were on the phone, and there were five phones outside, some of the prisoners would plug their stereos in there and turn the music up loud while you're on the phone. If you told them to turn it down it would end up in a big fight. A huge fight. And they never forget either. They're like a pack of dogs. They don't forget, but you give them a coke token and they'll come over and offer to turn the music down. It was just more peaceful. It's weird what they'll fight over in there. They'll steal your prison clothes that are the same as theirs, but you might have a newer jumper, it might be a bit bluer than theirs. They'll steal your toothbrush or your hairbrush or your shoes.

Everybody in there gets the same sneakers but you might have a newer pair than them so they want yours. It's just ridiculous. They just want what you've got even though they've got the same stuff. They fight amongst themselves, they fight with you, they fight with anybody who's around, they don't care.

It was funny because the gardens officer was a contractor. Although she's a prison officer, she's on a contract, and the other officers used to pick on her and make her cry all the time because she was nice to me and some other people. She used to give me phone calls from her office and they weren't allowed to do that. She was quite upset a lot of the time at work. So much bullying. They used to say that she's too close to us and they don't like that. She's still there. I went back there and saw her. I was in the area one day and I decided to go and see her. I shouldn't have done it because you're not allowed to have any contact with them. I rang up the gatehouse when I got there and they answered, 'Banyup Women's Prison.' I recognised the voice but I couldn't put a face to it. I said, 'Can I get put through to Ms Night's office, that's the gardens officer.' He said, 'Who's speaking?' I quickly made up a name and said, 'I'm from the forestry, I've got seedlings that need to be delivered to the prison.' 'Oh yeah, no worries, I'll put you through.'

She answered the phone and said, 'Ms Night speaking,' and I said, 'Hello.' Do you know what she said? She said, 'Get fucked!' She used to swear a lot. She said, 'Get fucked, is that you?' 'Yeah.' 'How are you? How did you get put through to my office?' I said, 'I rang up the gatehouse.' She said, 'Get fucked, you haven't changed, have you? You're not allowed to do that.' I said, 'Well, you answered.' 'I did too, didn't I? Get fucked!' This was only a couple of years ago. Suddenly she said, 'Where are you?' and I said, 'Sitting outside the prison. What time are you finishing work?' She said in half an hour. She said she'd walk out to the car park and have a yarn with me. She walked out and she gave me a big cuddle and asked me how I was going, because she'd had breast cancer too. There were two officers who had finished work for the day and they came out. One of them said, 'How are you going, Annette?' 'Yeah, alright.' He looked at me and he went, 'Awww, you rang the gatehouse, didn't you?' 'Yep.' 'I thought I recognised that voice, I put you through, didn't I?' I said, 'Yep.' He said, 'Oh nooo.' It was good to catch up with her, but I laughed, that 'Get fucked!' Nice lady, I think without her it would have been so much harder. I liked her, I had a lot of conversations with her about stuff. I had some dark times in there, sometimes I'd say, 'I can't be stuffed working today, I'm depressed.' Digging all those holes, mowing all those lawns, putting all that fake lawn down, moving all that dirt, it was ridiculous, it was like being in the army.

CHAPTER EIGHTEEN

The Underbelly

There are many ways to commit suicide in prison. You can cut yourself with razors you buy from the shop, you can hang yourself. There was a lot of self-harm going on in there. They push you right to breaking point where you just don't give a shit anymore. I had some lonely, dark hours there. The scariest place I've ever been in my life is my own head. You start believing your own bullshit, your head starts playing these games with you. It's hard to pull yourself together, you're just walking around like this empty shell.

I was never afraid for my own safety, I just thought, what can they do to me? But I've seen some pretty hectic fights in there. Some of those people are like walking time bombs. And you know who they are. They're fine one minute and the next they just trip out. They start throwing things, they fight, they start yelling, suddenly you're getting yelled at for no reason, you just look at them.

There was a man there, Fred Smith, who was head of security. He just had this thing about me. He also knew I was Ted Murcott's daughter. He used to put me down in isolation all the time. Just for looking at him. I used to get thrown in isolation a lot for doing nothing.

Isolation was just a room with a toilet, no toilet seat, there's a shower in there and a bed and that's it. There's nothing in it. You can't have a radio, TV, smokes, nothing, you just sit there. There's nothing you can pull off the wall, there's no way of harming yourself, you just sit there. They stick your little food tray through a little slot thing and every morning Mrs Martin, the warden, would come, and they'd open the cell and she'd want to talk to you. You'd have to stand up like you were in the army and after a while you'd have to say sorry for your behaviour and I'd say, 'I'm not saying sorry.' I might be in for a week then. And so it would go.

'Stand up, Mrs Martin's coming. Say sorry.'

'No, I'm not saying sorry.'

'Stand up, Mrs Martin's coming.'

'Who gives a fuck about her, I'm already in isolation, it can't get any worse. What am I apologising for? I'm not even supposed to be in here, why am I apologising to her?'

'Well, maybe you can have a couple more days down here.'

'Good! 'Cos if you thought I liked my other room, I really like being in this room, this room is my favourite and so I don't have to put up with you, or the yelling and the screaming, or the rest of them out there.'

'Well, you can spend a few more days in here.'

'Good, I love it in here.' And they'd just slam the door.

What they wanted was to punish me, what they didn't realise was that it wasn't punishing me, it was giving me peace. The yelling and the screaming goes on all day and all night. About seventy-five per cent of the prisoners yell, and they fight, and they bully and they just don't shut up, and the language that comes out of their mouths is just horrendous.

Lisa and I were often put down the back. She tells it like this:

> And then we had problems with security who didn't like us. We spent a lot of time down the back. Humour helped get us through even though it got us into even more trouble. I used to call Annette my n....r. We had these knitted 'chain' bracelets and we used to pretend that they were two-way radios, and when security was taking us down the back for something we hadn't done, we'd put our wrists up to our mouths and say, 'Yep, onto that,' and 'Are you receiving?' and security, [Fred Smith], would start screaming, 'I've had enough of you!' and he'd totally lose the plot over our stupidity. We'd get a laugh out

of that, seeing him so pissed off while we were going down the back for nothing.

We got put down the back and kicked out of the good unit for, in his words, 'the good order and management of the prison', because 'our stare intimidated him'. This is the person running a prison, the boss who'd been in the prison system for twenty or thirty years. Intimidated by me and Annette!

We could have physical contact with our kids if it suited him and if he didn't decide to throw us down the back just before our visits.

The kids could put in gate mail at outcare at the front of the prison and they'd go through a gate and then come into the visitor's area. They could put gate mail in, which we were supposed to get that night, and he used to withhold our mail. I'd phone my mum and she'd phone my lawyer because it's a federal offence to withhold the mail. Mum put in an official complaint for me against Fred Smith and suddenly I got mail in bulk, three months' worth of kids' mail.

Little things like that would piss us off so we'd do stupid things to piss him off, nothing bad, but after he told us it was for the good of the prison and because we intimidated him, we got an egg carton and cut two sections out and made glasses out of them with pipe cleaners. Then we stood at muster with these goggles on. Everyone was laughing at us and we said, 'Well, we're not staring at him now.' We'd make one like a bloodshot eye so it looked like a drunk eyeball hanging off a pipe cleaner, just to amuse ourselves. So now we weren't staring at him and he chased us around the basketball courts screaming, 'Right, you two, you're going down the back!' He obviously had the prisoners laughing at him chasing us around the basketball court and we just thought that was hilarious.

I told all of this to the court when I was taken before the CCC (Corruption and Crime Commission) when they were investigating him, and he was demoted from there because of that, and because he was having a relationship with a prisoner. We knew about that and we worked out later that this was the reason he was attacking us all the time, because we knew something we shouldn't have.

Miss Christie was a lovely older woman who, if she was on nightshift when we were down the back, would let us out to make phone calls so we could talk to our kids. She knew what was going on and that we were being unfairly treated, so she'd unlock us and quickly sneak us to the phone, then quickly lock us back up again. A couple of times she objected to our treatment and I assume she had something to do with me being called into the Triple C, but I don't know. All I know is that it was more than one person.

Without each other it would have been very lonely.

They give you anti-depressants like a sleeping tablet in there. I said, 'I don't want this stuff, I can't take this stuff. I'm depressed because I'm in here.' They'd say, 'It will help you sleep.' But that wasn't what it was about. They said I needed to take it to slow my thoughts down, but I thought, I know what you're doing. It was ridiculous. And they'd make me take it, too. You have to take your medication when you're in the medication line, and you have to lift your tongue up and poke it out so they can make sure you've taken it. You're forced to have it and then they started giving us this Largactil, a yucky liquid stuff. It's an anti-psychotic drug used for schizophrenia. We'd stand in the medication line and Jen would say, 'Right, are you ready for your Shut the Fuck Up Annette?' That's what she used to call Largactil. We'd take it and then we could hardly get back to our rooms before we were practically crawling on our knees onto our beds. They used to decide when we got that.

They used to tell me it was because I was going to have a big, huge court case and I needed it. It makes you slow down, it makes you not care anymore. You can't remember stuff. It affects your memory. I stayed on the Largactil for the rest of the time I was in there, until about six months before my court case. I told them I wasn't going to take it anymore but they tried to force it on me. They told me they'd force me, that they'd just hold me down and they'd administer it by needle. They'd drug you up, then you'd go to work and you couldn't work properly. Twice they held me down and gave me a needle.

Everyone has to see a psychologist. When I told Susan, the psychologist, about the Largactil, she got angry. She said, 'Why haven't they told me about it?' I don't know who put me on it but it wasn't her. I don't know who it is who decides that. After my court case, she phoned me at Dianne's place. You're not allowed to have any contact with any of these people when you leave there. She was just ringing to see how I was going. I'd become quite friendly with her during my time in prison. You get an hour with them, and to start with, I didn't used to say anything, I'd just sit there and she would sit there, and I'd sit there, I think she was waiting for me to start the first conversation. That went on for a long time. A couple of months, maybe four months later, I started talking.

Meanwhile there was the psychiatrist, Sam. He's the one who prescribes the medication in there, I think. I only saw him once or twice. I remember seeing him and I mentioned the antidepressants and said I didn't want them. I told him that everyone was on them and he said I shouldn't be on them at all because the problem I had was that I was stuck inside a prison. Apart from that, he said, you're smart, you're intelligent, there's nothing wrong with you, it's because you're in here.

I also don't know what the side effects are, all I know is that it made me tired, I couldn't be bothered arguing a point or anything, it just made me not care about anything anymore. I didn't even care if I got no visitors.

My grandmother got ill while I was in prison. She asked to see me and eventually I could visit her in hospital. It was a big drama getting permission. They didn't want me to do it. It involved requests from me, my mum and my lawyer plus lots of paperwork. I was handcuffed to one of them and my legs were shackled, and a chain was attached from the shackles to the handcuffs on my wrists. I was then taken in a big Ames truck with two officers to see my grandmother. They parked on the road across from the hospital so we had to walk across the main road to the main entrance. It's all about humiliation. There were a lot of people around just staring at me. When I walked into the room, my grandmother began crying. She said to them, 'Would you mind taking these chains off my granddaughter?' It was embarrassing, seeing my grandmother for the last time in that condition. They said, 'No we can't, ma'am.' She said, 'My name is not ma'am, my name is Mrs King.' That was quite funny, I had a bit of a chuckle there. Mum was there too. I was only allowed fifteen minutes with her and she died a few days later.

It was difficult to get to her funeral, lots of forms to fill out. They make it hard. They only allow you to stay for twenty or thirty minutes and you can't stay for the gathering afterwards. They make sure they pull up right in front of everybody and I was handcuffed to a security officer. It was the first time I met Dianne's husband. It was all pretty awful. I had to sit beside Mum right up the front and she was crying and I couldn't hug her or anything because I had some arsehole cuffed to me. There were relatives that I hadn't seen since I was ten years old or even younger. Aunties, uncles, cousins, they were all there and I was handcuffed. It was humiliating. I spoke to them but wasn't allowed to have real conversations, I wasn't even allowed to have a drink and it was the middle of summer. Ross asked if he could get me a can of coke but he wasn't allowed to, they were afraid someone might put something in it. I wasn't even allowed a glass of water. As soon as grandma was cremated, I had to go. The humiliation I felt was intense, and I hadn't been convicted of anything, I was just on remand. It was cruel.

Even now, I don't know, when I get really angry, which doesn't happen very often, I'm not too sure of what I'm capable of because I've got a lot of that inside. It doesn't happen anymore but while I was in prison and after I came out, for a while I'd feel this intense anger sometimes. It's a horrible feeling, you don't know what to do with it. It's a build-up and you can feel it coming but there's no outlet for it. So, you start yelling and throwing things. I don't like arguments. I can't handle them because I could boil over very quickly. It doesn't take long to go from being very placid to extremely angry in a very short time. I don't like it. I was never like this before I went to jail. It changed me.

K said one day that if I was a boxer I'd kill someone in a boxing ring.

My sister Dianne says I should go to anger management. My family hasn't seen me like that – I don't have arguments or get angry with them, although they did see that side of me when they visited me in jail because I would just get so frustrated. When you want to see your lawyer and you want to get out of there and your lawyer says he'll see you next week and you don't think he's doing anything and weeks will go past; and to communicate with someone on the outside and you only have ten minutes and you keep getting cut off by the officers if they don't like what you're saying on the phone, and writing letters that are blanked out by liquid paper because they don't like what you're writing, it's frustrating. There's no way of communicating. You want something done about it and it seems like it's not happening. What are all these people doing? You're in there and you want out and it's not their fault, they can't do anything to speed the process up, but you want out of there. You feel helpless and enraged.

So I'd say to Mum, 'I want out of here now! I can't be in here. You don't know what it's like, it's terrible.' And yet the other people in jail seem to accept that they're there and they seem to be having fun. I don't see what's fun about it. But I suppose they are there for a reason and they know it. I was there and I'd done nothing wrong. And the friends that I had there had been sentenced. They used to say to me, 'What are you so upset about?' and I'd say, 'It's alright for you, you know that you're going to be here for two years, or three years, or four days. I'm still waiting to see what's happening. It's a completely different scenario. And you did those things you did – I didn't and I want out of here.' But you can't get out. And you're constantly thinking of ways to get out. And you get treated like you've done what they're accusing you of. You get treated worse by the officers because you're not being accused of stealing a chocolate from the local deli, so they've already formed an opinion of you because of all the media and everything, which is all rubbish. One minute there's a story saying I confided in a good friend, which is BJ, and another story says it was a man I didn't even know. So, what is it? Did I know that person or did I not know that person? It's so hard to let go of it. Everyone asks me why I don't just let go of it but I can't, it's just there all the time.

I went to anger management when I was in prison but it was ridiculous. I don't lose my temper now. I can control my anger by controlling my thoughts.

When your lawyer comes to visit you at the prison, he'll give you paperwork about the court case and he'll have it in yellow envelopes and you'll take it back to your room. The staff are not allowed to have that paperwork, but this one time my lawyer came and I don't remember why but I couldn't see him so he left the paperwork at the gatehouse. He said to me later, 'Did you get the paperwork?' 'What paperwork?' 'I left you some paperwork there, it's got a sticker on it saying it's from your lawyer and they're not allowed to open it, it's confidential.'

It would appear that that paperwork went all around the jail, all the officers were reading it and about five days later it ended up at admin. 'Annette, we've finally found your paperwork.' It had been opened and read. And so, I asked my boss at the gardens, Leanne, if she had a shredder because my lawyer told me to shred it after I'd read it, so I started memorising it then shredding it all. When I went to court, BJ had files and files of paperwork. I didn't take any to court with me. I knew what those witnesses were going to say because I'd read it. I used to say to Mum and my lawyer, 'How am I ever going to remember any of this when I go to court?' But I found that when those people took the stand, I knew what they were going to say as they were saying it, because I could remember what was said in all that paperwork for some reason. I've never remembered anything like that in all my life.

When I got to Bandyup, they kept on swapping the trial dates. First it was for six months after I arrived and a trial date had been set. I'd go to court for a hearing, one of those days when you're just there for ten minutes or so. They'd say, 'We've set a court date for such and such a date,' and the prosecution would jump up: 'We're still waiting on paperwork or this or that.' My lawyer would go, great. They'd set a new court date. Three months later we'd go to court and they'd change the trial date again.

It was supposed to be in Broome and about three weeks before I was supposed to go up there, they changed back, and then they changed it back to Broome again. My lawyer said it's not a very good idea to have it in Broome and he wanted it changed back to Perth.

So I'd waited all that time and I found out six days before I was supposed to get in the truck and travel the twenty-two hundred kilometre trip up to Broome. I think the reason they wanted it in Broome was because the Peter Falconio case had just happened. My lawyer didn't want me tried up there because everyone knew about the case and he said I wouldn't get a fair trial and that was probably the reason why the cops were pushing for it to be up there. My lawyer asked why it couldn't be in Perth, saying it makes more sense since I was in Perth. They responded, no, we want it in Broome, and I think they would have come down a lot harder up there. I believe he was right – if I'd gone up to Broome I think they would have set me up. Broome's a six-hour drive from Port Hedland, a lot closer than the almost eighteen hours from Port Hedland to Perth.

Then, just before my trial, before I was supposed to go up to Broome, I got cancer.

CHAPTER NINETEEN

Cancer

I'd been in prison for about sixteen months when I got cancer. It was the longest stretch of time in my life. I told my mum that in there two weeks passes like it's two months. There was nothing to do, no oval or anything, just a basketball court in concrete city. And it was so emotionally exhausting. I used to get these headaches all the time. I thought it was from thinking too much. There would be days when I would be so depressed I even thought about killing myself. I told my mum, I just can't do this. They make you go to work and you can hardly scrape yourself off the bed but you must because they kick you out of your room. They just don't care. Even my friends would sometimes ask what was wrong with me. I'd say, what do you think's wrong with me? It's alright for you. You've had your sentence; you know when you're getting out. I'm looking at a life sentence. A life sentence in this fucking hole!

When I first went to prison, I said to Mum, 'Something bad's going to happen, either to me or to K.' I had this feeling about it. She didn't know what I meant and I said, 'This is going to be my punishment.' She said, 'You're being ridiculous, it's just something playing on your mind.' I said, 'I bet you I get cancer or something happens to K.' She responded, 'Nobody in our family's got cancer, don't be ridiculous.' I thought I'd be punished for leaving the scene with K, for not doing something.

I was working in the gardens, which was hard work, and I'd been there a long time when I started getting tired in the afternoons and feeling really irritated with people. Even after work I didn't feel right and I'd want to go and lie down, I'd feel exhausted. I said to one of my good friends, 'There's something wrong with me. I don't know what but I just don't feel right.' I was just tired and angry. I thought it was maybe just being in there, it was emotionally torturous. Then I started thinking I had cancer although I didn't know what it felt like to have cancer, and then it got worse. I also had pain in my shoulder. It felt sore from under my armpit and into my shoulder, right inside my shoulder. I told Mum during a visit, but she told me, no, it was just the court case that was coming up.

For about six months, I started feeling unbelievably tired, felt irritable and started getting these massive headaches all the time. I would flare up and get angry without too much to set me off. People started noticing how moody

I'd become. By then I was working in the kitchen from six in the morning until twelve with a couple of hours off until two when I was supposed to go back to work. I just couldn't do it. I wanted to sleep instead and be on my own. The noise in that place was horrific, with people screaming and yelling all the time, so I wanted to find somewhere quiet. Sometimes, when they locked us out of our units, I'd have to go and lie down on the concrete somewhere – just to find a little peace. It would never last long.

Before the cancer symptoms kicked in, I'd normally go and play a bit of basketball or volleyball but then I got snappy with people when they kept asking me to play. They couldn't understand that I was tired and, eventually, I just said, 'Fuck this, I'm going back to my bed.' They'd follow me up there and hassle me. 'Come on, don't be stupid,' they'd say. 'What's wrong with you?' I'd tell them to leave me alone. Of course, they were upset by this. One of them was my friend, Lisa, and the others were pretty good friends. Everyone was confused by my behaviour. 'There's something not right with me,' I said to Lisa one day. Like Mum, she thought I was upset because the court date was coming up. 'No,' I said, 'I think I've got cancer or something. I'm going to die.' She really thought I was joking. Everyone thought I was being stupid and told me not to be ridiculous.

I told Mum what I thought and she asked me why that would be. 'I think I'm being punished,' I told her. 'I've always known that something was going to happen to K or me as punishment for me not staying when Bevan died. I told BJ he'd done it and had to deal with it, and I left, so this is karma.' If there was a God, he was going to make me pay. Am I religious? No! But, strangely enough, when Mum then suggested that maybe I should go to church, I said, 'I'm not going to church. After what he's done to me, I'm not speaking to him anymore.'

People became unintelligible. I'd see their lips moving but couldn't make sense of what they said. 'You're talking shit,' I told Lisa. We'd both crack up laughing so it was hard to convince her that something was wrong. It was as if I couldn't listen properly and what people were talking about was rubbish.

After about five months, I said to Lisa, 'I can't handle this anymore. There's something really wrong with me. It's getting worse.'

I put the form in to see the doctor and told her that I was tired, irritable, and that I had cancer. She told me I was being ridiculous.

They found a lump under my arm and suggested that it was just a cyst. But I knew it wasn't something simple like that. 'I want to go to the hospital,' I said. They must have thought something wasn't right, because a couple of days later I was sent to the Royal Perth Hospital for tests.

I knew, just from their expressions when they looked at my ultrasound. They went and got the specialist who looked at it and said he thought I had a cyst. I said, 'No, I've got cancer, haven't I.' 'No, it's probably just a cyst,' he said again. But I knew from the look on his face that he didn't believe what he was saying. Fuck, I thought, I knew it. I'm going to flaming die.

They did a biopsy and they came in and told me I had cancer. I wouldn't have had the surprised look on my face that they expected. 'Yes,' I told them. 'I know.' I was already prepared to hear it, but that didn't make the news any easier. I suppose I'd been hoping all along that I was wrong. Thinking about K and wondering what was going to happen to him growing up without a mother. Those thoughts kicked the fear right out of my head. And it was those thoughts that scared me – not the cancer. I felt angry and ripped off by God, even though I still didn't believe in him. He was the only one I could blame it all on. I guess when you haven't really done anything wrong, but had plenty of bad things happen to you, you need to find someone to blame for what's going to happen to your son. K didn't deserve anything like that. I couldn't blame Bevan – he was dead. And BJ had plenty to deal with himself.

They did a blood test and said, 'One of the most aggressive cancers we've ever seen. It's gone through your lymph nodes. Giving you chemotherapy and radiotherapy isn't going to make any difference; we'll do it but it won't help.' They said they were sorry and wished they'd got me in earlier. They told me it was caused by stress with my body breaking down.

A huge black pit had opened at my feet. I felt hollow. The tumour was the size of my fist. And then all I could think of was: I've got to go to this trial. I had to go back the next day when they said they'd give me surgery, chemotherapy and radiotherapy. They implied that it was wasting their time but that they felt obliged to do it. I said, 'I can't do that, I've got to go to a trial. I've got to go to Broome, I can't do this now, I don't have time for this, I need to get out of jail.' This was all that was in my head, I don't have time for this cancer thing because I need to go to court to get out of jail.

My mind was on repeat. Over and over, thinking the same things – K, court, get out of jail. Everything kept spinning around to the same point – K, court, get out of jail. Maybe my crazy, round and round thoughts were keeping my brain from fixating on the cancer. The black pit was still there at my feet, waiting to swallow me up. But I ignored it. If I was going to die, I had to think of other things. Thinking of K and the court case gave me hope that something good might happen. But then we talked about what the doctors had planned. That wasn't good news.

The doctors told me that they would do the surgery first, followed by the chemotherapy, then the radiation. They wanted to cut my boobs off. I was looking at some photos and thinking, that's not going to happen. 'I'm not going to do that, I am NOT doing that!' I said to them.

'It makes more sense to me, and I'm not a doctor, but why can't you do the chemotherapy first and then do the radiotherapy and surgery last?' They said, 'Because that's not how we do it. We do surgery first then chemotherapy then radiotherapy,' and I told them I didn't want to do it like that. They said, 'What?' I told them, no, I just wasn't doing it.

They wanted me to sign a paper saying this is what we're going to do and I told them, 'I'm not doing that, I don't want to do it. I need to go to court first.' They said, 'If you get on that truck to Broome, you'll be dead before you even get there.' I said, 'Well, I want chemotherapy first.' They said, no, they don't do it like that. I said, 'Well, I'm not doing that, I'd rather die.' 'OK,' they said.

There were doctors over from America who said, 'OK, you can be the guinea pig, but you have to sign a piece of paper saying this is what you wanted,' and so I did. I did the chemotherapy first and when they came to do the surgery, which they did before the radiotherapy, they said, 'I don't know what you've been doing but there is no sign of you ever having cancer.' So, they didn't cut a tumour out, they cut out the cells around where that tumour used to be. And they took my lymph nodes out because it had already gone through my lymph nodes. They told me that I'd have to do all this physiotherapy, that I'd never be able to throw a ball again, that I'd never have proper movement of my arm or shoulder again. But there's nothing wrong with it now.

I've got bigger muscles on my right-hand side even though I'm left-handed. You can see this on my chest X-rays, the muscle that goes across the right side of my chest is quite big because I was exercising that shoulder more when working in the gardens. I suppose if I want to stretch my arm up to the sky there's a bit of a pull on my shoulder. It still hurts across the right side, across the top of my chest, it aches sometimes, but I've had that looked at and it's just scar tissue. I have an annual check-up, sometimes more if I don't feel well. Every time I get sick, I think I've got cancer. They said I didn't get any punishment – well, this was my punishment. I'm square with the house now. I've paid for taking off. To this day, I've got a seventy per cent chance of the cancer coming back. So, why do I still smoke? I really don't know the answer to that. Maybe it's my defiant nature, or me sticking my middle finger to a brutal and unfair God that doesn't exist.

I thought I was going to die and I wouldn't be allowed bail. I thought I was going to go back to prison for the rest of my life. All those officers would say to me, 'You may as well get used to being in here 'cos this is where you're going to be for thirty years.' So I told them, 'If I go back there, I won't have chemotherapy or radiotherapy, I'll just die, so you won't have me either way. I'm not staying here. Either I get out or I die from cancer. You're not having me.'

They'd say, 'Get used to it, Murcott, 'cos nobody gets off that charge, you're not innocent. Everybody says they're innocent, but there's not a person in this jail system that's innocent.'

I had chemotherapy every two weeks and radiotherapy every day after that. They wouldn't let Mum or anyone else visit me. I kept saying to my lawyer, 'I'm going to get out of here.' He'd say, 'You will not get off a wilful murder charge. You need very exceptional circumstances, I can't even put a bail hearing in, they won't take it. You need something.' I said, 'I'm dying of cancer.' 'I didn't expect that,' he said. It sounded on the phone like he had tears in his eyes. I'd become close to my lawyer – he was the best, he was like an angel to me. He came and saw me the next day. He said, 'When I said exceptional circumstances, Annette, I didn't mean that.' He said, 'I've put a bail hearing in.'

Three weeks after I'd started chemotherapy, I went to court for the bail hearing. I had chemotherapy in the next two days or so and they double-dosed me accidentally for my weight and they nearly killed me anyway. I ended up being rushed to emergency; well, I don't think they were in a big rush, because they gave me chemotherapy for a person with a body weight of eighty-two kilos and I was fifty-two. I thought I was going to die that day.

When I went to the bail hearing, the prison sent the bloke who runs the medical board of the prisons. He fought the bail. He claimed that I'd be better off in prison and they'd look after me better. I just stared at him. The prison didn't want me out on bail, the prosecution didn't either. But I think the judge had already made his mind up. Maybe he could imagine his own wife in my situation, I don't know. My lawyer said, 'We want bail on exceptional circumstances,' and the judge said, 'This is not exceptional circumstances, this is *very* exceptional circumstances.' But the bloke from the prison lied and lied and lied. On the morning that I went for bail, Mrs Martin, the warden, came and saw me. She said, 'I hear you're going for bail. You won't get it, there's only one person who's ever got it for wilful murder in the history of Australia and that was back in 19xx, but you want to hope you get bail.' I said, 'You want to hope I don't.' She said, 'I'll see you when you get back.' I said, 'No, you won't be seeing me because I'm not coming back.'

When I was in prison they weren't looking after me properly because you're supposed to have medication in the morning before you go in for chemotherapy, and they wouldn't give it to me. When I needed to see the doctor, they wouldn't let me, and when they double-dosed me with that chemotherapy, my temperature was huge. I didn't know about the double-dosing and I said to my friend Lisa, 'I'm going to die.' The hospital had told the prison that if my temperature went over a certain amount, I needed to be rushed to hospital emergency immediately. Do you think they'd let me go anywhere? They wouldn't even let me have a phone call. So Lisa rang her mum to call my mum, and my mum phoned the prison and they hung up on her. Then my mum rang my lawyer and my lawyer rang the Royal Perth Hospital and the hospital rang the prison and said, 'You'd better get her here within the hour or otherwise you're going to have a death on your hands,' and then they started moving their arse. I couldn't get out of there, I couldn't get to hospital, it was like some ridiculous movie.

Finally, I got to emergency and they said, 'What's happening? What took you so long to bring her?' They were running around trying to get blood tests because it kills all your blood cells but they couldn't get a sample because my veins were collapsing. They said, 'You need to ring her parents,' but the prison wouldn't let my parents come to me at the hospital. So, they stuck a dirty great big needle in my groin. I remember saying to them, 'God, I wish I was dead.' I just wanted to die, I didn't care anymore. I wasn't allowed to have any visitors, not one. They wouldn't tell my family I was at the hospital. They kept on talking about me all the time and every doctor and nurse that came in there wore masks so *they* wouldn't give *me* germs. Then my lawyer burst in the door and they told him he couldn't be in there. He told them he was my lawyer. He just looked at me, then spoke to me a little, then he said, 'I'm going to get you out of there.'

So I had to go to court and get an adjournment and they had to tell the court that I had cancer and all these doctors were there and there were letters to the court saying there was no point in this person going to trial because she's going to be dead before she even gets there, and the prosecution said, 'OK then, we'll wait until she gets better.' They said, 'She's not going to get better.' The prosecution said, 'We'll wait and see then.' BJ's lawyer said, 'Well bugger this, we'll just get on with this trial. We don't need her because he's said that he did it. We'll just split these two up, he can go to court for wilful murder and we won't worry about her.' The prosecution said, 'No, we're going to wait because we're going to try these two together.' My getting cancer extended BJ's time in prison.

I had my treatment and they waited and they waited and they waited. I had the chemotherapy, the surgery and the radiotherapy, and about a week after that was all finished, I went to court. I was as sick as a dog.

In court, they lied and my lawyer questioned that bloke from the jail and asked, 'How did Annette get from the prison to the hospital?'

'We took her there.'

'How did she get there?'

'In a Commodore. As we do when people need special treatment in these circumstances.'

I thought, liar, because I went in one of those terrible trucks.

My lawyer continued, 'So she went in a Commodore?'

'Yes, because she was very ill and we take care of,' and blah, blah, blah.

'Was she handcuffed?'

'No, we wouldn't do that, she's on remand and she's got cancer, we wouldn't do that.'

'Oh, so she went in a Commodore, and when she was in hospital was she cuffed to the bed?'

'Oh no, we don't do that.'

'What would you say if I told you that I came and visited her when she was in hospital?'

'Well you didn't because she wasn't allowed to have any visitors.'

'Well, I've got video footage of her in the hospital bed handcuffed to the bed, then that chain went to an officer, and she was shackled, with chains around her ankles, and then shackled to the bed. What would you say if that happened?'

'Well no-one went there.'

'I'm just going to put this video on.'

And the judges said, 'Bail.' They said, 'Animals get treated better than that.'

My lawyer had asked, 'What does she do in jail now that she's got cancer?' 'She gets out and she goes and plays basketball and she's out mixing with her friends,' they replied. I thought, liar. As soon as I got cancer they locked me in the medical centre, in a room, in virtual isolation.

I almost never saw daylight, I could go out and see my friends one hour a day, no-one was allowed in to visit me, I wasn't allowed to make phone calls, I wasn't allowed to do anything, I was just locked in that room. I remember one of the nurses saying, 'I can't do this.' I was angry then. I was having chemotherapy, my hair was falling out, I wasn't allowed to see anybody, it was just so bad. When I got out of the hospital and was taken back to the prison, I was taken to administration where they check you out to make sure you haven't put a phone up your bottom or your vagina or whatever they think you're smuggling in there, and they said I'd have to go through to the medical centre because they had to check my temperature. There were a lot of officers there.

I said, 'I'm not going back to my room, am I?'

'Yeah, we'll take you to the medical centre then take you back to your room.'

'No, you're going to lock me up in the medical centre.'

'No, we're not going to do that to you.'

'Yeah, I know you are.'

'Well, you're very sick.'

'I'm not sick.'

'Yeah you are, you're dying.'

So, they locked me up in the medical centre. And that's where I stayed. In a room. That's where they gave me my dinner. I could do nothing, just sit in that little room.

I did get on with some of the officers. One of them, Leanne Night, had had breast cancer. She was my boss in the gardens and she became like a mate, we became friends. The other officers used to treat her like shit because she used to get on well with me and quite a lot of the prisoners. They used to pick on her, belittle her and talk about her. It was bad. They were a bunch of bullies.

Mr Lawler, the prosecutor, was one who was always good to me. I always went to him if something happened and he'd always come. Mr Miller was quite a good officer. There were a few of them in there. The rest were just wankers. The female officers were the worst. Ninety per cent of those officers in there should not have been in that job. They were mean and vicious and treated you like you were less than nothing. When they put me in that room, Mr Lawler was on holidays. They said, 'Mr Lawler's not here now, Annette, what are you going to do about it?' I said, 'Go in there and die. Don't mind if I do really.' It was a disgusting thing to do to someone but that's what they did, left me in the medical centre.

When I was granted bail, I was released that day. My mum was there, along with some friends. It was school holidays so Mum and Dave had K, but Dave had taken him to get a milkshake so he wasn't in the courtroom. When I walked out of the Supreme Court in Perth, K and Dave were walking up the footpath towards the court, and K came running and jumped into my arms. It was an emotional moment, it felt so good, but there were cameras everywhere. I was looking right at the cameras thinking, 'What are they taking photos of?' There's a photo of me with my parents and there's a photo of me holding K's hand but K's not in the photo.

They told me that once I'd finished my chemotherapy, I'd have to go back to jail to wait for my court hearing. I told my lawyer that I cannot spend another hour in there. I can't go back. He told me there was nothing he could do to stop it. He said, 'I can ask, but I've already been told, they won't let you out on bail after your treatment, that was the deal, you get let out on bail until you get better, even though you weren't supposed to get better, you were supposed to be dead.'

The whole prison experience was emotional torture and I hated them for the way they treated me and others.

CHAPTER TWENTY

BAIL

I vividly remember the night before bail was to be pulled. I was at my sister Dianne's place and I thought maybe I was having a bit of a nervous breakdown or something. I said to Dianne, 'There's something wrong with me.' I was feeling sick, I was jittery, my whole life was flashing before me and I was thinking, this is it. This is the end because they'll probably pull bail and this is the last time I'll have my freedom.

I ended up going to the Joondalup Hospital in northern Perth. I went up to outpatients and they asked me what was going on. I told them stress. It felt like I could feel my heart beating in my neck. It was bad, I couldn't stop crying and I told Dianne, 'I can't do this, I'm not going there,' and she said, 'Well, you can't run away from it.' I was thinking, I'm not going to turn up, I'm just going to nick off. But where am I going to go? I don't know, I'm going to go somewhere, but I'm not going there. My mind was spinning through all this stuff. I had to be at court the next morning at nine o'clock and they were going to pull my bail and then set a hearing date.

I was a mess. I couldn't hold a thought, I was worrying about K and thinking, 'What happens if this is as good as it gets, right here, right now. What happens if This. Is. It. and I'm going to go back in there for thirty years. And for something that I hadn't even done. I was so distressed. I didn't understand what was going on. It was like it wasn't real, like it was happening to somebody else. It felt like being in a dream, like, is this happening? But it is, but it doesn't feel like it is.

It was like I was watching my own life, but it wasn't happening to me. It was terrible. I was dry-retching and vomiting.

When they asked at the hospital what was wrong, I told them I had this big court case coming up. They gave me some sleeping tablets and other medication and I went back to Dianne's place with her. I think she must have rung up my mum because my stepdad came down from work. I didn't know he was coming and he pulled into the driveway and he walked in the doorway and he looked at me pointedly and said, 'I want to talk to you for a minute.' I respected him heaps and he was that bloke who I never wanted to disappoint. He stood by me all the way, he was such a good person to lean on. It was too hard to talk to

Mum because I suppose it made me attached to it. He was as well but not like Mum.

I went outside with him and he said, 'What's going on, mate?'

'I can't do this. I don't want to do it.' I was crying.

'I'll tell you something,' he said. He was a mine manager at the time. 'I look at work and all these hard things I have to do and I look at how hard my life's been, and then I think of you and whenever you think you look up to me, I want you to know it's actually you that I'm looking up to. You're one of the strongest people that I've ever met in my life. You can do this. You need to do it for your mum and for K.'

'Yep, and what happens if I don't leave tomorrow from court?'

'You'll do the time that you have to do, it's as simple as that.'

I was so upset. I said, 'I was thinking of nicking off.'

He said, 'Don't you dare!' I was sobbing uncontrollably. 'We'll see you tomorrow morning 'cos we're picking you up at eight o'clock.'

I think he suspected that and that's why he came. I think my sister told him. And he probably knew anyway. My lawyer had already told me, because they have to really, 'You know you're going back, don't you?' I said, 'Yep.' He said, 'I can't stop it because your treatment has finished now. You knew that this was coming.' I said, 'Yeah, but it doesn't mean I have to accept it. How do you accept that? I haven't even done anything. It's bullshit.'

That night I went out and had drinks. My friends were good that night, telling me they were going to miss me. They were trying to talk me into believing that everything was going to be alright, but I knew it wasn't. I got drunk and when I went to the bail hearing the next day I didn't feel very well. That night I could hardly sleep, it was toss, turn, toss, turn. I woke up in the morning and my mum and Dave were there. My sister couldn't stop crying. K was with his dad. I'd told him I was going back to court and that I might be going back to jail until my court case, and he was so upset. I said to him, 'I'll see you soon,' and he said, 'OK.' Then I thought, bloody hell, how am I going to pull this off? 'I'll see you soon.' Why did I even say that?

Mum, Dave and I drove to the court; Dianne couldn't handle it. We parked and my brother Ross was standing there. I said, 'You're a sight for sore eyes.' I was so glad to see him. We'd always been good mates and now we're good mates, close. My lawyer was there and he told me I had to go through certain doors and hand myself in and then I could go into the courtroom from there. I told him I didn't want to. He said I had to and I said, 'Why can't I just walk into the court with you and my mum and Ross and Dave? Why do I have to hand myself in, what difference does it make? I've still got bail until I walk in there.' 'OK then, I can't stop this, they're going to pull your bail.'

They've got an area like a big oval there, a big lawn area and I looked over at it and he said, 'Don't!' I said, 'What?' He said, 'You're going to run away, aren't you?' I said, 'I was thinking about it. Mmm.'

So I walked into court and sat next to my brother until they called me up and I sat up in that little area where your lawyer stands and where they talk to you. Then the prosecution got up and said, 'You know the deal was that once she'd finished chemotherapy and if she survived, bail would be pulled. We didn't think she was going to survive, but now that she's still here, we're asking for her bail to be pulled until the court date.'

I was thinking, this is fucked. My mum was crying and my lawyer said that he was prepared for it, and he knew this day was coming, and so on and the judge just said, 'No, I'm not going to pull her bail. She hasn't broken any of her bail conditions, we've got a fifty-thousand-dollar surety, she's sick and I'm going to keep her out until the court case.' He said to the prosecution, 'Hurry up and make a court date because it's getting ridiculous. These people have been on remand way too long. Come up with a court date and no more excuses.'

My lawyer said to me later, 'That would be a first in court history, I reckon.' And they set a court hearing for two or three months later.

The prosecution objected to the decision and of course fought it. I was a flight risk, I was a murderer and so on but the judge had made his decision. I felt so good. There was suddenly no hangover then, I just thought, 'Yes! This is getting better.'

We walked out of the court and I went down and stayed at Mum's place. I was still on bail and so still couldn't leave the house before eight o'clock in the morning and had to be home by eight o'clock at night and I had to sign in at the Bridgetown police station every day. K came down and we hung out. We went fishing and friends would come down and stay. My other sister was living down there and we had lots of family time. It was good.

CHAPTER TWENTY-ONE

Trial

But the court date came around and I was again feeling anxious. I had to stay in a hotel with my parents in Rockingham, south of Perth. The hotel was close to the Supreme Court and I wasn't allowed to go outside that room. Every morning I went to court I had to go into the courthouse and the police would take me downstairs and lock me up until I had to appear, and then at lunchtime they'd take me back down and lock me up again, then at the end of the day I'd leave the court and go back to the hotel. The case lasted two weeks.

The prosecution's case was that I had asked BJ to come over and kill Bevan. They claimed we'd both killed him while he'd been asleep on K's bottom bunk. They said that BJ and I were having an affair.

During the trial, people would make their presentations and say the most outrageous things and I wasn't allowed to talk. A lot of the witnesses the prosecution called up helped us more than they helped them. Others were just ridiculous.

They put a bloke on the stand who said I'd gone to his house and asked him to kill Bevan. I didn't even know where this guy lived. I had no desire to either, he was a junkie and I've always avoided people like that. My lawyer cross-examined him and worked out that I wasn't even living in Port Hedland at the time he said he met me and used to see me all the time. We were still living in Newman at that time.

There was a witness who said she lived a few houses up and across the road from me. The police would have gone doorknocking and got statements. She said she knew me, that we'd had conversations and she'd seen me down at the shop quite often with black eyes and looking beaten up. She said that on the night Bevan died she heard a sound like a T-ball bat hitting concrete. I recall my lawyer asking:

'In your statement, Ms X, you don't mention anything about a T-ball bat. Why is that?'

'No, I did mention it. They wrote it down, I remember. I told them it was a metal pole-type thing.'

Her smile was indicating that she was enjoying the attention. But then she began to frown.

'In your statement you said, "The noise was like metal hitting the floor. Kind of hollow sounding." There's nothing about T-ball bats or pipes in your statement. Is that right? Do you remember that being part of your statement to the police as it was three years ago? Since then, did you hear from the media about a bat being part of the incident?'

'Everyone did, plus lots of other things.'

She made it up. My lawyer basically told her that she'd changed her story over time because of what she'd learned. That frown dragged all the way down to her mouth which was shut firmly like a clam.

She was totally discredited. Same as that other bloke. People I didn't even know. He thought he'd give a statement but he didn't know they were going to come back and make him jump on the stand. Small towns, everybody wants to get involved with something. When police go doorknocking they should have to tell people that this is going to be a big court case and they could end up in court. These people didn't think about that. The whole trial was just a crock of shit.

The reality is, there was a fight and somebody accidentally got killed in self-defence. It happens. But to them it was this wilful murder case that was planned by everybody, planned by K's dad, planned by my brother, planned by everybody I'd ever known and everyone was in on it, especially me. I don't understand how that happens.

Then there were the professional witnesses, the forensic experts and so on and they were interesting.

There was a police constable who did forensics, particularly fingerprints. None of those prints connected me to this incident. I remember my lawyer telling the court:

'It's curious. If she was presumed to be involved in this homicide then you would think her bloody fingerprints would be everywhere. There were none to be found on her at the time nor on the victim that would link her to this incident. And that's because she wasn't involved.'

How can something like this be ignored? My lawyer was making it glaringly obvious.

The evidence of the forensic scientist from the PathCentre backed up my and BJ's stories. She said there was no contamination on my clothes or in the house that connected me in any way to the killing or the removal or touching of the body, simply nothing.

They had found the t-shirt I'd been wearing and that I'd thrown on the bed when I changed, and tests showed no blood on that, but they found my blood on my shorts from when Bevan had backhanded me in the car on the way to BJ's.

Another expert's evidence also indicated that Bevan had to be mobile and moving around during the fight, as there were blows to the front and back of his head, not just one specific area, so the prosecution claim that he was lying asleep on the bottom bunk was a fabrication. She said if he'd been on the bed, he would have ended up with a fractured skull, which he didn't.

This particular expert had not seen or heard BJ's account of what happened but when BJ's lawyer questioned her, she agreed that her findings were the same as BJ's story of what happened. I remember my lawyer saying:

'This expert very methodically went through her reports of all the samples that were provided to the PathCentre. Not one piece of forensic evidence analysed by her team connects my client to the killing.'

Then there was a blood analysis bloke who had been on courses and lectured in interpretation of blood spatter and bloodstains but made no sense at all. In his summary, the judge told the jury to totally disregard his evidence 'in its entirety'. I remember the judge addressing the court:

'Any individual who comes into the court and presumes to be an expert in blood splatter and throws around opinions about using trigonometric calculations without explaining how his opinion is reached must be disregarded. You will remember that he had examined several stains which he thought were bloodstains, however, we now know that some of those stains were not. Anyone who has knowledge of mathematics would know too well that you cannot calculate the trajectory of a particle through air using trigonometry.'

The judge went on to say that in a recent decision of the Court of Appeal, the court had had to order a retrial in a case where this blood analysis guy gave evidence in a similar case to ours, because his 'evidence' was dodgy.

And then there were the police witnesses. The prosecution tried to downplay the aggression and abuse I'd been dished out by Bevan. They said I'd exaggerated it. But the police had to admit in evidence the time Bevan was arrested and taken down to the police station. Bevan had got into a rage and it took four of them to restrain him. One of them was Ron Billets, I never forgot him. He arrived with another officer, a sergeant, around six o'clock one evening. That was the time Bevan damaged my HiLux. In the incident report, one of the coppers said Bevan wasn't the sort of bloke you wanted to have to confront on your own because he could see that there was a storm brewing behind his eyes. They had to call in extra police to control him. He'd hit one officer but he never got done for that, assaulting a police officer. Same old story. I remembered my lawyer questioning a sergeant over that night:

'How many police officers were used to detain him and prevent him from leaving?'

'There was Senior Constable Ron Billets and myself. Later another sergeant showed up.'

'I'm looking at this report and it suggests that you had your hands full with him. It says, "[Bevan] threatened police and tried to push them aside. He tried to hit an officer before being held back by the arms." Is that correct?'

'Yes, it is.'

The sergeant's body language suggested that he didn't look too bothered, but every now and then he'd look my way.

'It then says, "He tried to get away and became aggressive. After a while he was threatening and abusing officers. When he was placed in handcuffs after three or four minutes he continued his rant." Did it really take that long to place the handcuffs on him?'

'Yes, it did.'

'It goes on to say that, "[Bevan] inflicted minor cuts to the police officers' hands but no other injuries." Nothing else?'

'No, there wasn't.'

'As I mentioned, it appears you had your hands full with him. Is that correct?'

'Yes.'

My lawyer checked his notes before continuing with the questions.

'A few months later, we're looking at around end of March 2002, you were called out to a domestic disturbance. Is that correct?'

'Yes, that's right.'

'And with this incident you noted that Annette Murcott had deep cuts on her nose and bruising?'

'Yes, she did.'

'Apparently this was from a head-butt?'

'She told me it was a head-butt and how she received it.'

The sergeant looked at me again but only for a brief moment before being dismissed from questioning.

Then they called another policeman, a constable, to the stand. He'd come around to our place with another copper once when we were living in Newman. Bevan had thrown a beer stubby at me. This policeman said he didn't talk to me because he was dealing with Bevan while the other copper was talking to me. He wasn't allowed to say what my complaint was as it would be 'hearsay' as I hadn't told him directly, I'd only told the other copper who then told him. He said I had no injuries and no charges were pressed. Then BJ's lawyer got him to look at the incident report which clearly said that I required medical attention. They had wanted to take me to hospital but I had refused.

The police were questioned about records which they said they'd lost when they were moved from Port Hedland to South Hedland station, or at some other unknown time. I recalled he asked this constable:

'It says here that your statement wasn't prepared until 10 September 2003?'

'Not sure, maybe not.'

'I take it that it was after [Bevan] died that you then had to think back on these incidents?'

'Yes.'

'So you prepared a statement in case it may be questioned in these proceedings?'

'That's right.'

The constable swallowed hard and his shoulders started to tense.

'Is it true that you were aware that there were other occurrences involving Annette Murcott and [Bevan] before you went there on 9 November 2001?'

'Yes.'

'You may or may not recall that there were four previous incidents?'

'I don't remember the exact amount.'

'Do you recall that on one of those call-outs a sawn-off shotgun had been discovered at the home belonging to [Bevan]?'

'No. This is the first time I've learned of this.'

I thought he had delayed his response.

'Are you sure? You don't recall that incident?'

'No, I don't remember. It's not something I would forget.'

I wasn't convinced. He began shifting in the seat.

'So you didn't check a database when Annette's mother phoned you to check on any previous issues to learn what was happening?'

'I only spoke to the officers at the station and enquired about their dealings with them, that's all.'

'So no-one at the station who had dealings with [Bevan] informed you of the finding of a .22-calibre sawn-off shotgun?'

'Like I said, I don't recall.'

My lawyer pointed out that it would seem most unusual for police to go around to an incident without doing a check to see what they might be walking into. It's basic safety really. And I note that at the end of 2001 they were called to our place for the fifth time and we hadn't even been living there for a year at that stage.

My lawyer also questioned them about other records and whether they'd been purposely lost. There was the incident when Bevan had bashed up my sister's partner and left him unconscious, and he'd gone to the hospital and had photos taken. He wanted to put Bevan on an assault charge. There's nothing to say that that ever happened. It's all gone. Bevan's dealings didn't exist anymore. My lawyer said:

'I find it very odd that there are all these incidents involving [Bevan] admitting he was a violent man, you're admitting now that he committed domestic violence, that he was found with an unlicensed firearm with a hundred rounds of ammunition, where did that go? Where has all this stuff gone? It seems very convenient to me.'

After we were halfway through the trial, my lawyer started saying to me that their story was falling apart. He said, 'I think you're going to be alright. I can't say one hundred per cent, but their story isn't making any sense. The jury aren't going to believe it.'

Then I went on the stand and my lawyer later said, 'I was a bit worried about you at first, but I couldn't have picked a better witness.' He said I was a bit nervous and jittery at the start but the more the prosecution started hammering me, the worse it became for them because I wasn't nervous or anything by then. There were lots of people in the courtroom and two prosecutors so it was a bit daunting at first, but after that first day, I wasn't having it. They try to intimidate you, they stare at you and they talk to you like you're a piece of shit. I thought, I'm not putting up with this. They'd tell me to look at the jury when I was talking. They had almost thirty witnesses for the prosecution in court. Witnesses to what?

There are only three people who know what happened there that night and one is not here. Witnesses to say what? That I smoked Winfield Blue cigarettes. I said, 'Yeah, I do.' They asked me if I was denying that. Why would I deny that? It was insane. They made up a story of what happened and they tried to make me believe the story. If they had you in jail long enough and then said to you, 'We're going to give you thirty years in prison but if you plead guilty we'll give you five years, you'd probably go with their story just to not have to stay inside, you can see what they do.

BJ was sitting next to me throughout the proceedings. We said hello as we were walking into court from the lock-up area.

He said, 'How have you been?'

I said, 'Just great.'

'How's K?'

'Yeah, he's doing OK.'

'I just wanted to let you know that I'm sorry.'

'I know you are.'

'No, I am. I'm really sorry. If I could change it, I would.'

'I know you're sorry.'

'I didn't mean to do that.'

'I know.'

'Maybe in time you can forgive me.'

'Maybe, I'm not sure. Not sure.'

A part of me has forgiven him. It's hard to forgive him for the time I spent away from K, but he didn't do it on purpose. If he'd gone in there with the intention of doing that, it would be unforgivable, but at the same time, I have to ask, would I still be here if he hadn't done it? If that didn't happen that night, would I still be here? I don't think so.

I did say to him in court, 'I want you to fix this, because I'm tired of it. I need to go home and be with K.' But he was already telling the truth and always had been. He admitted to everything in court and told them everything that had happened. And he repeatedly said, 'She had nothing to do with this. She had nothing to do with this.' They said that we could have put a story together and BJ started laughing. He said, 'This happened in a split second in somebody's life. We didn't have time to talk about it straight after it happened and we haven't seen each other for a couple of years, we've had no communication apart from a couple of letters from prison which had nothing in them, how could we come up with a story?' Our stories were exactly the same, down to the last detail, and they were exactly the same story because it was the truth.

Now for the voire dire.

Recently Dianne sent me a link relating to my court hearing. It was the record of a voire dire, which is a hearing to determine the admissibility of evidence, or the competency of a witness or juror. This voire dire was held in the Supreme Court in Broome in June 2004, the year before the trial. BJ and his lawyer didn't want certain statements used in evidence in the trial. These were statements that police claimed he'd made to them while he was in Roebourne prison where he was held after the murder.

BJ had had a couple of video interviews after the police picked us up that night and there was also a typed written statement that he'd signed. A couple of months later when he was in Roebourne, two coppers, Cop 1 and Cop 2, decided to drive two hours to go and interview him again.

They didn't tell BJ they were coming and they didn't know if he'd even talk to them. They didn't take any video recording equipment with them and they knew the prison didn't have any. They could have driven ten kilometres to the Roebourne police station to get a camera but they didn't. BJ said he'd talk to them anytime so they interviewed him. Cop 1 took handwritten notes, and then BJ signed them.

BJ said they never mentioned anything about videoing it. He never said he did not want to go on video. He also denied there was any talk about him receiving legal advice about giving a statement. He thought they were just clarifying everything he'd said to make sure it was correct. He said he signed the piece of paper 'because I was asked to'. He thought that he, Cop 1 and Cop 2 were friends and he trusted them. He did not know he was signing a statement and he didn't read it before he signed it.

A month later BJ went to the South Hedland court for a hearing. When it was over, BJ was waiting in the holding area to be loaded into the transport vehicle when Cop 1 came over and asked him to sign a typed copy of what he had signed in May. He started to sign and then read about two-thirds of it and found it was full of lies. He told Cop 1 he was not going to sign it. He objected to particular paragraphs and Cop 1 said he was going to remove them and reprint it. Cop 1 took it away but by the time he returned the prisoners were being loaded onto the truck and BJ didn't see a revised version.

Among the points that I remembered that were in this statement that BJ claimed he didn't say were:

1. 'Don't recall the exact words but Annette insisted I go with her to the her house and help kill Bevan.'
2. That I told him to 'kill Bevan', and
3. That I handed him the baseball bat.

The judge ruled the evidence inadmissible.

It was also mentioned in the voire dire that BJ was given his typed statement to read and sign, but he got angry as he read it, saying he was being set up, and wouldn't sign it.

They were trying to set me up and that's why I ended up in jail. This was the start of a nightmare. This is why I'm saying that case was built on lies. Yes, no-one denies BJ killed Bevan, but not in the way they said. No-one conspired anything, it was a fight that went wrong. That detective, Cop 1, I will never forget his name or face, he made my life a nightmare, and why? I did nothing to Bevan, and BJ did not intend to kill him.

They used that interview to upgrade my charge from accessory to wilful murder. BJ didn't say those things and that's why they didn't video it, so they could add in their lies. And that's why I ended up in jail. If I'd been charged at the very beginning with accessory or manslaughter, I would have been out on bail all that time. They upgraded the charge so I'd be kept inside. It's the only reason I can see, because they had nothing to upgrade me on without that. Nothing. How they did that I don't know; I'll never understand that. They said to me at one stage, we don't know which one of you did it, and I was thinking, come on, yes you do, you know. BJ was admitting it. Apparently, people admit things like that all the time, but I don't know what kind of people do that.

I tell people, be careful what you wish for, because I would sometimes wish Bevan was dead, I'd wish he would die, because he was right on the verge of killing me at times. So many people say that Bevan got what he deserved. It was frustrating in court when the prosecution was absolutely drilling me and not even listening to what I was saying. One of the prosecutors, there was not one but two, got me so wild at one stage, saying you did this, you did that, what did you do in that seven minutes, and what did you do in that three minutes? I said, 'Hang on a minute, this is going back two years eight months. Here we go again, you're asking me something but you're not listening to what I'm saying.' And I'd be thinking, look at me not at the jury when you talk (she was looking at the jury), you're not hearing a word I'm saying. You've made up this whole story, this is what's happening. It's *not* happening, I'm not having it.

She said to me, 'This person stands here with no remorse.' I thought: fuck me dead. She carried on, 'You are not upset that he died, are you?' I said, 'I'm upset at *how* he died, but I'm not sad that he died.'

CHAPTER TWENTY-TWO

Verdict

Before the judge sent the jury off, he reminded them of what penalties the different charges could bring, and he also said, 'Remember, this is two people, these are their lives,' and I think that opened the jury's eyes up a little bit. I found the jury hard to read.

I had the feeling by that time the judge was getting annoyed with the prosecution who were turning up late all the time. They'd roll up ten or fifteen minutes late. And they'd just bring up stupid things, like when I was on the stand I remember them asking me:

'You smoke those Winfield cigarettes?'

'Yeah.'

'Yeah, well, we found your cigarette butts at the house with your DNA. So you can't refute that.'

I thought, how ridiculous is that? No-one's denying I smoke Winfield Blue cigarettes, for God's sake. It was absurd. I think they were trying to build up a picture of me and it wasn't meant to be a good one. Then I remember them asking:

'You smoke marijuana, don't you?'

'No, I don't.'

'Your friends do, though, don't they?'

I was being scrutinised and belittled, from things on the radio, in the newspaper, then in court. My whole life was on display and they were painting this horrible picture of me because Bevan had died. And you can't say anything about it, I'm just standing there like an idiot in the court having to listen as they said horrible things about me. I'm not a bad person, I'm not a bad mother, I'm sorry about how he died but I had nothing to do with killing him.

Some people advised me not to look at the jury, not to stare at them, but I couldn't help it, they were straight across the room from me. I'd try not to make eye contact with just one person, I'd try to cast my eyes across them. I remember one jury member who kept on staring at me all the time. I don't know whether it was a disapproving look or what it was so I tried not to look at him too much. I couldn't help looking at them because my belief is that you should look at people when you're talking to them. I wasn't looking my best because I had short hair. I'd been sick, of course, but they weren't allowed to know that so they wouldn't feel sorry for me. That was never brought up.

My mum was the last witness to take the stand. Because she was a witness, she wasn't allowed in the court. She was very upset about this and she had to sit outside every day while Dave was inside. She was also upset when she took the stand. I'd rung my mum on the night of the murder and they wanted to know what was said, and she told them. After that she could stay in the court and listen to the summing up and the verdict.

The jury went out a bit before four o'clock and came back in around lunchtime the following day. I felt sick during that wait. My lawyer just said it could go either way. It was an open court and the room was packed. I was called back in about lunchtime. I felt terrible, very emotional. I was crying, it was really stressful. You have no idea what they're going to say until they say it. I felt sick. I looked at my mum and she was crying too.

Finally, the jury came in and I remember the verdict was read.

The Clerk of Arraigns said something like, 'Do you find [BJ] guilty of murder or manslaughter or not guilty?'

The Foreman replied, 'We find him guilty of manslaughter.'

Then it was my turn. I was shaking.

The Clerk said, 'Do you find Ms Murcott guilty of murder or manslaughter or not guilty?'

The Foreman replied, 'Not guilty.'

My heart was pounding. It wasn't over, was it?

The Clerk said, 'Do you find her guilty or not guilty of accessory after the fact of manslaughter?'

The Foreman replied, 'Guilty.'

I thought, oh no. This is ridiculous. This takes me with him, because whatever sentence he was going to get, I was going to get. The jury then went and sat down in the courtroom behind Mum. One of them said something to Mum like, 'I hope she gets off.' I could see Bevan's brother there, he's the spitting image of him. Then the prosecution asked the judge for the longest sentence for manslaughter which is twenty years. My heart sank. It was just getting worse. My lawyer said he wasn't happy with that, he didn't think it was appropriate.

The judge sentenced BJ to four years and eight months' imprisonment backdated to 3 March 2003 and so he was eligible for parole. He went back to prison where he spent one more month while he waited for parole, which he was granted.

When the judge sentenced me, he told the court that he had the opportunity to impose a merciful sentence and that's what he intended to do. He said that I had suffered very considerable trauma as a result of Bevan's death and subsequently. He also said it may have been that the stress and violence in my relationship with Bevan may have caused or contributed to my cancer.

He said I had served eighteen months in prison already and so he would give me a sentence but suspend it from that day for a period of two years, and so I was free to go.

When the judge handed down the sentences I cried. I just couldn't hold it in, it was such a relief. There was a stir in the room, I heard Mum yell out, 'Oh, thank God!' or something similar. There were a lot of happy people, including some of my friends. Everyone was talking and crying and they yelled out to me, 'Congratulations,' and 'I can't wait to see you.' Mum called to me, 'Well done!'

Then I had to go down to the lock-up area because my shoes were down there and I had to sign some paperwork for my release. My lawyer said he wanted me to come outside with him. I said no, I wasn't going out there with all those reporters there. He insisted and when I asked him why he said that it would be good publicity for me, so I walked out and Mum and Dave were out there already.

There's a good photo of me and my lawyer with Mum and Dave in the background. My lawyer gave me a hug and then the press came up and were asking me questions. They were right in my face. They asked me if I had anything to say and I said, 'It was just an unfortunate event which I wish had never happened.' They asked me what I was going to do now and I said, 'I'm going home to be with my son.'

K saw that on TV. He was with his dad, waiting in the hotel. We arrived outside the hotel and all my friends were there with bottles of champagne and Dave was crying and

Mum was crying. There was that big oval-like lawn and I could see K and his father walking across it. I think I was in a bit of shock. I was so happy and had a big grin on my face, it was a lot to take in.

Every day during the trial I'd have to wait outside the court and the prosecution would walk past and they'd always make some remark. 'You're not getting away with this,' or, 'We're going to get you for this.' I'd always say, 'You're not actually, I'm not having it.' They'd reply, 'We've got way too much evidence, you've got nothing.' I was getting angry by then. I saw BJ before we went down to the lock-up to sign the paperwork. He said how sorry he was about everything. He hoped one day he could catch up with me and K. Again he said he was sorry and again I told him I knew he was. He was a very quiet and gentle man, and he was very relieved. Like me he'd been told no-one gets off that charge, you won't be walking out of there, and there he was, twenty years reduced to time served.

CHAPTER TWENTY-THREE

Aftershocks

That first night of freedom was a big night. Everyone got stuck into the champagne. Mum wanted to take me back home to her house. I think she was babying me a bit, understandably.

I didn't think about the future too much that night until K's father asked, 'What are you going to do? You want to take K, don't you?' I said yes, and he said he didn't want me to take him. I said, 'You've had him all this time. I want him now, he's mine.' K's father said, 'He's not just yours.' I knew that, but I wanted him, and K wanted to come with me too. K's father suggested he stay with him until the end of the school year. At that moment K didn't like the idea and was jumping all over me and didn't want to let me go, but that's what happened. He stayed with me for the next couple of weeks of school holidays, then went back to his father. It nearly killed me, I hated it. He was a bit torn about going back. I think he wanted to be in two places at once.

On the second day after the trial, I went down to Mum's place. I was feeling pretty crook after that night. K wouldn't leave my side, he was like chewing gum on the bottom of my shoe. We spent a lot of time at the river and fishing. It was always when I went to go somewhere, like down to the shop, he'd be on to me, 'Where are you going?' 'Just down to the shop.' 'Oh. I'll come.' I couldn't get rid of him and I'd be sitting in the lounge room and I'd think, I'll just go outside for a bit, and up he'd jump, he'd come too. I'd just be going out to have a smoke, and 'Where are you going?' 'Just out for a smoke.' 'You're not going anywhere, are you?' 'No, I'm not, I'm here.' He'd always have his eye on me. It was as if he had eyes in the back of his head. Poor little bloke.

A short while later I moved down to Perth. I still had radiotherapy and more chemo to go through, so I did all that, six months or so of chemo which I had to go in for every second week, and then four months of radiotherapy which I had to go into the hospital for every day. I was staying with Dianne in Perth during this period. I'd been having daily radiotherapy throughout the trial as well. Every single day I had to drive to Royal Perth Hospital. It was a pain in the arse and I didn't want to do it.

You're supposed to go to counselling but I didn't want to go, I didn't want to go and sit there talking about cancer to all these people I didn't know. I suppose I was trying to distance myself from it. In my mind, the less I thought about it, the more it was going to go away. I told them I wasn't going and I wasn't dying that day or the next day or the next and so I didn't want to know about it. Sometimes I used to sit there and think, holy crap, this is happening. But I was alright with that, I wasn't scared of death. I'd think, well, Mum will be OK eventually, their lives will go on, but how does K grow up without his mother? That was the worst thing about it, it used to play on my mind a lot.

This is going to sound crazy, but when I had cancer and there was a chance I'd die, I was afraid of meeting Bevan again if there was an afterlife. I was always worried about that; I didn't want to see him again. I still feel that. Just in case there was an afterlife, imagine that! It would be horrific. It's weird, it didn't matter what the doctors were saying, 'We can't help you, you're going to die,' I knew in some part of my mind that I wasn't going to, and even when I was going to court, I had this feeling that this can't be it, I'm not staying in jail for the rest of my life, I'm not here for that reason. I've always thought that I was here for a reason but I just didn't know what it was. Lots of people say that, and I've always thought it. Even now I think, my God, I don't think I was put on earth to drive a dump truck, there's more to it than that, there's something more to life than this.

When I was being hurt by Bevan, I felt emotional pain as well and it was hard to deal with, but I suppose because I had K, I had to pretend that wasn't happening.

I have a very high tolerance to physical pain now. It's the emotional pain that will bring me to my knees every time, guaranteed. If someone hurts me, I feel this deep sadness. I suppose it takes me a while to forgive somebody and it takes longer for the pain to go away than it normally would take. It cuts very deeply with me.

There was no moment when I thought: I've made it, I'm not going to die. I don't even think now that I'm going to be OK. I've got a seventy per cent chance of getting cancer again so every time I get sick, I think I've got cancer. I do believe that eventually I will die of it, but I'm OK with that, I'm not scared. Obviously, I don't want to leave K but I've never feared dying.

When the radiotherapy finished, I needed to get a job. K was still up with his dad. I spoke to K about it and he wanted to be with me, but he wanted to be with his dad also and I didn't even have a house. I got a job driving dump trucks with Dave who was mine manager out at Cataby Mineral Site, a mineral sands mine. You don't need a police clearance unless you're working on a gold mine, but still, I was lucky that Dave was manager.

I rented a house in Jurien Bay and the mine was a hundred kilometres away. I drove to and from work each day which became very tiring, so I got a house in Moora where I stayed for eight years. My parents bought that house for me to live in, and that was only sixty kilometres away from the mine. After a year, another company took over the mine and so I found another job up in Eneabba, but I had to drive up and stay for two weeks, then drive home. K went to boarding school so he could stay on in Moora. He was thirteen at the time and after a shaky start, ended up loving it.

I didn't like Eneabba very much, I hung on for about six months there, then moved on to the Mount Gibson iron ore mine near Geraldton. I'd drive the two hours up there and work for two weeks – one week of day shifts and one week of nights – then drive back to Moora for a week off, then head back to Geraldton and do it all over again. I learned to drive monster trucks at Cataby after I got out of jail. These trucks hold three hundred ton and these are the ones I'm still driving now. But working on a mine feels a lot like being back in jail.

K and I are in touch every day, usually just a text or a quick call. He tells me, 'I just want you to know that I love you so much.' I say, 'Yeah yeah, I know and I love you so much.' And I still have the message on my phone from when he said, 'I want you to know that nothing you ever do will ever make me embarrassed, for everything you ever do I am so proud of you.' I have heard from so many people how very caring, loyal, honest, hard-working, and very, very loving he is. He and I are very close. He has such a nice soul. Although I tell him I'm alright, he sees my sadness. He's the only one who fixes it for some reason, I don't know why.

Bevan had a son – there was a photo on his fridge but he hadn't seen him since he was about two years old. He was about six when I met Bevan, but Bevan hadn't seen him for a long time and I knew there were some issues with him and his partner, I know that he used to bash her. A couple of years after the court case I was living in Moora where I had moved in 2007. I got a letter from a lawyer saying that they wanted compensation for all the maintenance he'd missed out on. The son would have been about eighteen by then. This was a boy that I'd never had any contact with, Bevan had never had any contact with, and I thought, great, this has reared its ugly head again. I called my lawyer and told him about the letter, I sent him a copy of it, and he told me not to worry about it. He took it to court and nothing came of it, I never heard anything else.

It took me a long, long time to get over all this stuff, the court case, my family getting hurt, and people don't understand the depth of that pain. I hear, 'Oh just get over it, you'll be right, when are you going to get over this?' Especially my mum: 'Well, we're done with that now, get over it.' So I suppose I dealt with that internally, which took a huge toll on me. It was pretty bad.

Even now when I think about it I get this pain in my stomach and in my heart. Even now, it's a very touchy subject. Whenever I think back on things, tears come to my eyes. It brings back a lot of pain. It's like a burden in my life. It's almost like an old friend, that's what I call it. When I think about it, I say, 'Hello, old friend,' and it's weird because your life can be going along fine and then all of a sudden it comes back and it just destroys you again. And then you're picking up the pieces of your life again and then things go along fine for a while and then that comes back. I don't know what it is, depression maybe, this thing that comes and goes. It's the only thing I reckon that drops me to my knees in my life, it's like a shadow over me all the time. If it ever goes, I probably won't know who I am. I say to Mum, it's like some horrible bear that awakens all the time, and I can feel it coming and I try to push it away but I can't. It comes most often at work, where I think I've got too much time to think. At other times, it can come when I've been happy, maybe for a couple of weeks, and then it just arrives and I might be unhappy for a day or a week or a month. People notice it and ask what's wrong. When I ask why, they say, 'You're not laughing anymore.' I tell them I'm OK. I never felt like that before all this happened, it wasn't part of my nature. I don't feel angry, it's a sad feeling deep inside and the only person who fills that is K.

I've been studying to get a project management qualification. It includes health and safety which had also been part of the horticultural courses I did while I was in Bandyup. I have to go and see my lawyer and get a police clearance, I'll have to go to court to get rid of the note about imprisonment on my record. It comes off after ten years, but because the trial went through the Supreme Court, you have to apply through the court to have the note removed from your record. With any record you can usually just go to the police station to apply for it to be cleared. On my record it doesn't say I was just in there on remand, it says imprisonment for X amount of time. It doesn't say that I was waiting to go to court. It makes it sound as though I'd been convicted and sentenced to prison.

CHAPTER TWENTY-FOUR

Regrets

I was just thinking about K's dad. He was the love of my life and I suppose I'm always looking for what we had. There's a sadness I carry around inside still when I think about him. K is a daily reminder of what once was, and how young and stupid I was not to take my mother's advice: 'You don't know what you've got until it's gone,' and then I was too pig-headed to go back.

Anyway, I still get a lump in my throat every time I think of him or us, and when I talk about him. I don't know why, maybe because it wasn't supposed to end. It's one of my life's regrets and that, my friends, is a fact.

K said to me once, 'Have you ever known what was going to happen before it happens?'

I said, 'Why is that?'

'Sometimes I just know things that are going to happen and it comes true.'

'Do you?'

'Yeah, do you ever get that?'

'Yeah, all the time.'

It's hard, because you know what's going to happen, but you don't want it to happen, and you can't change it. It's a burden and people call it a gift. They tell me I need to work out how to use it, but I just think, you can have it. It's a burden. I don't know if it's something I'm meant to be using in this life, or if it's a punishment, I'm not sure. I don't know. K doesn't feel it as a burden. We don't talk too much about it as I don't want him to feel the way I do about it.

He's asked me where he got it from, me or his father. I said I didn't know, maybe a bit of both. I told him it's like angel whispers. It's like when you know a fence is electrified and you go to touch it and a little voice says, don't do it, but you do it anyway just to see what happens, knowing you're not supposed to. It's that little warning voice in your head that you ignore. I don't ignore it anymore. Probably everyone's got it, it's that little split-second voice that says, don't do that! It might be nothing extreme, not a life or death situation, just that little, tiny thought that you have that you go against. And everyone says, I wish I'd done that, I wish I'd done what I thought to begin with. As I've said to K, it doesn't matter how much you're in love with someone, that thinking of the heart just doesn't exist to me, because the thinking of the mind is saying: what are you doing? That isn't the right thing to do!

The night Bevan was killed, I said to BJ, 'I don't need you to come around and make sure I'm OK, because no good's going to come of this.' I absolutely knew it. I knew it. I also knew I should never have gone home that night, I knew that no good was going to come of that and I told BJ that. I knew when I saw BJ standing over Bevan and he said, 'He's dead.' It was like there was a dead silence. It was like the silence after a cyclone – I've been in a couple of cyclones, Cyclone Olivia in Pannawonica, Cyclone Bobby – it was like that. Everything stops, and it turns around and it comes from the other direction and that's when you know you're in the eye of a cyclone. And I just knew that this was so bad, but I had K in the car, and I remember BJ saying 'I've killed him,' and he was vomiting and everything, and he said, 'Do you think we should ring an ambulance?' and I said, 'I don't know, because you did this, I'm leaving now.' That was the last conversation I had with BJ that night. Because it's sort of like you either sit here and deal with it, or, I think a lot of it is adrenaline, the fight or flight mode thing, you're either going to fight or flee and that's what I did with my son.

I said to my mum, 'Whether what I did was right or wrong, and if I get punished for it for the rest of my life, at least no harm will ever come to K again. No-one can hurt him anymore.' And for me, that decision to flee was the right thing. It was the right thing for my son but for me, probably not. Looking back on it now, I wouldn't have changed it. It wouldn't have mattered if I'd done a lifetime in jail, or thirty years or twenty years, there was no way in the world I was going to have an ambulance there, police there, my son there, all this terrible thing going on, I just didn't want to do it. So, if that's a bad thing to do, then I'm guilty of it.

CHAPTER TWENTY-FIVE

Unfinished Business

About three years ago I woke up in the middle of the night and phoned BJ. He answered the phone and said, 'Hello, Trouble,' and then, 'How's the little man?' which is what he used to call K. I said, 'Really good. I wouldn't mind catching up with you because this is just terrible.' He said, 'One day we will. One day.'

www.ingramcontent.com/pod-product-compliance
Lightning Source LLC
Chambersburg PA
CBHW030254010526
44107CB00053B/1709